D1008716

Most books about boards are yawns. The few that are readable often lack substance. *The Imperfect Board Member* is unique in that it is both captivating and truly helpful. Every leader should read it.

—Bill Hybels, senior pastor, Willow Creek Community Church and author *Courageous Leadership*

Governance is a vitally important topic that commonly comes across as agonizingly dry. Hurray for *The Imperfect Board Member*—a rare and refreshingly enjoyable book that cleverly mixes an entertaining story with memorable principles that are practical, insightful, and incredibly comprehensive. It's a marvelous blueprint for governance excellence that is sure to be helpful to every board member on their journey to becoming, if not perfect, then extraordinary board members.

—Al Hatton, president and CEO, United Way of Canada

For too long, regulators and critics have presumed that tinkering with metrics like board size and director independence is the key to governance excellence. But it's not enough. Good governance is the product of skillful board members working well together with a solid grasp on the corporate strategy. In *The Imperfect Board Member*, Jim Brown captures this reality artfully. Read this book and discover for yourself the disciplines of governance excellence.

—Richard Leblanc, coauthor of *Inside the Boardroom*

The Imperfect Board Member is packed with learning for board members and those who aspire to be board members.

—Purdy Crawford, Counsel, Osler, Hoskin & Harcourt, LLP

Boards of Directors are a primary basis of trust for the corporate world and the non-profit sector. Sadly, that basis has been compromised in recent years—with predictable consequences. Jim Brown's *The Imperfect Board Member* is a tremendous book with an ideal prescription for a healthy board—and for increasing trust, the currency of the boardroom.

—Stephen M. R. Covey, author of *The Speed of Trust*

The Imperfect Board Member by Jim Brown is a highly perceptive, eminently readable, engagingly human book on how boards and directors can improve their performance. In a breezy conversational style that uses dialogue invitingly and often, the author explores with sensitivity and a light touch not only the standard ingredients but also the more subtle nuances of excellence in both corporate and not-for-profit governance.

> —William A. Dimma, author, *Tougher Boards for Tougher Times*; chairman, Home Capital Group Inc.

It's hard to overestimate the difference between an excellent board, a mediocre board, and a failing and complacent board. But all three have this in common: each of their board members is imperfect. What makes the difference? A clear vision of what a board is for, and how a good board functions. Jim Brown's new book is the best resource I know of to convey that vision. What *The Five Dysfunctions of a Team* does for staff members this book can do for boards—from charitable organizations to local churches to educational institutions to professional associations.

> —Brian McLaren, author of *A New Kind of Christian* and *A Generous Orthodoxy*

Jim Brown has delivered a business fable that is as provocative as it is unconventional. Do you know the Secret Formula for Organizational Effectiveness? Are you making the wrong sacrifice? Does the board lead with its nose or its fingers? *The Imperfect Board Member* presents these concepts in a manner that is both illuminating and engaging.

> —Scott Green, author of *Sarbanes-Oxley and the Board of Directors*

Being a good board member is often hard, unrewarding work. How timely that Jim Brown, a real student of the director's role, is sharing his best thinking. And how refreshing that he has embedded his wisdom in a compelling and entertaining story. You'll enjoy and profit from *The Imperfect Board Member*.

> —John Beckett, author, *Loving Monday*; chairman, R.W. Beckett

I've consulted with, served on, and even chaired boards in the profit and not-for-profit sectors for over twenty-five years. Most boards are well-intended, but confused at best, about their roles and responsibilities. I'm delighted to recommend *The Imperfect Board Member* to help board members and leaders to be confidently on-purpose.

> —Kevin W. McCarthy, author of *The On-Purpose Person* and *The On-Purpose Business*

Who needs a book about boards? As a CEO with over 40 years of experience in my business and hundreds of mind-numbing conferences and workshops on management and boards behind me, I certainly didn't think I did. But *The Imperfect Board Member* proved me wrong! This is an absolutely amazing book. It's a quick read. It drives home some stunning points, and it puts them together in an interesting and informative fashion. I have now read *The Imperfect Board Member* three times and I'm making a list of all the people I'm going give a copy to. The book is simple and understandable. The lessons are brilliant. WOW!!!

> —Ron Wettlaufer, general manager, Dufferin Mutual Insurance Company

An engaging story that works for family relations as well as board relations! Brown's clear and concise ideas put 'hands and feet' to solid governance principles. Not only will boards work better but so will staff. This book is full of applied wisdom.

> —John Pellowe, CEO, Canadian Council of Christian Charities

The Imperfect Board Member is a very easy read. It is of great value to anyone serving on a board, be it a private, public, or not-for-profit organization.

> —Hon. Lyle Vanclief, P.C., former Canadian Minister of Agriculture and Food; certified director, Institute of Corporate Directors

Not-for-profit and church organizations will be far more productive as they benefit from the insights in Jim Brown's excellent book, *The Imperfect Board Member*. All volunteers want to use their time to make a difference in the world. This book will help board members focus on effective principles and practices for their service contribution that will maximize their investment.

—Ken Bellous, executive minister, Baptist Convention of Ontario & Quebec

This is an interesting approach to learning more about governance. The parable is not only helpful to anyone involved in governance of an agricultural cooperative, but with family, family businesses, church, and community. It is an easy read and has a happy ending! This book can help make your life and the lives of those around you easier.

—Don Schriver, retired executive vice-president of Dairy Farmers of America and former chair of National Council of Farmer Cooperatives

Jim Brown brings passion, creativity, and results to the work he does helping leaders—I've had the privilege of seeing this first-hand in three different organizations. Now, in a fabulously fun book, Jim has created a tool to catapult new board members to great effectiveness and fine-tune the contributions of experienced directors. You'll want a copy for every member of your board!

—Bryan Hochhalter, senior pastor, Grace Community Church, Detroit

The Imperfect Board Member is a must-read book for every leader and board member who is striving for excellence. The concepts outlined in it provide an easy-to-follow road map to building a better board and a great organization.

—Ben Kubassek, author, *Succeed Without Burnout* and *Five F-Words That Will Energize Your Life*

THE
IMPERFECT
BOARD
MEMBER

*Discovering the
Seven Disciplines of
Governance Excellence*

Jim Brown

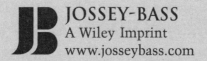

JOSSEY-BASS
A Wiley Imprint
www.josseybass.com

Published by Jossey-Bass
A Wiley Imprint
989 Market Street, San Francisco, CA 94103-1741   www.josseybass.com

Jossey-Bass books and products are available through most bookstores. To contact Jossey-Bass directly call our Customer Care Department within the U.S. at 800-956-7739, outside the U.S. at 317-572-3986, or fax 317-572-4002.

Jossey-Bass also publishes its books in a variety of electronic formats. Some content that appears in print may not be available in electronic books.

Library of Congress Cataloging-in-Publication Data

Brown, Jim.
   The imperfect board member : discovering the seven disciplines of governance excellence / Jim Brown.
      p. cm.
   Includes bibliographical references.
   ISBN-13: 978-0-7879-8610-0 (cloth)
   ISBN-10: 0-7879-8610-0 (cloth)
 1. Boards of directors. 2. Corporate governance. I. Title.
   HD2745.B735 2006
   658.4'22—dc22

                                                        2006019149

Printed in the United States of America
FIRST EDITION
HB Printing   10 9 8

CONTENTS

Foreword, Patrick Lencioni   ix

Introduction: Boards Matter   xiii

1   ON THE EDGE   1

2   A GLIMMER OF HOPE   15

3   THE SECRET FORMULA   27

4   THE ENEMY WITHIN   43

5   UNRAVELING FROM THE INSIDE   57

6   REBUILDING FROM THE GROUND UP   71

7   ONE STEP FORWARD, TWO STEPS BACK   83

8   EXPECT MORE   93

9   CATCHING THE WIND   107

CONTENTS

10 UNCOVERING THE GEM   119

11 BREAKTHROUGH   139

12 THE BIG DAY   149

Afterword: Making Application   157

Recommended Reading on Governance   193

Notes   195

Acknowledgments   199

The Author   203

FOREWORD

I t used to be that people looked up to boards of directors. They had no real idea what boards did; still, they trusted that these surely were honorable and important groups. But now that strange names like Enron and Sarbanes and Oxley have become a part of everyday language, the luster of boards has faded and the scrutiny of their work has increased. Unfortunately, most of that attention has focused on fiduciary responsibilities and legal liabilities, making it entirely likely that when all of this blows over, people will still be as bored with and confused by boards as they were before.

This is why *The Imperfect Board Member* is such an important book. In two equally important ways, it gives us a compelling look at how boards can truly add value, and along the way it shows us why boards are so important.

First, it makes the work of boards human. In spite of how boards are depicted in Hollywood, they do not consist of a bunch of cigar-smoking men in pin-striped suits sitting around in a dark, wood-paneled conference room figuring out how to deceive or manipulate naïve stockholders.

The truth is, most boards are made up of ordinary people. They are grandparents. They are Little League coaches. They are next-door neighbors. And they are often volunteers who have nothing to gain from sitting on a board other than taking part in a learning experience and knowing that they are contributing to something important.

Second, *The Imperfect Board Member* makes the work of boards entirely understandable and accessible. Sparing us the jargon that induces sleepiness, it provides a clear description of what boards should—and shouldn't—be doing.

This may sound like I'm saying this is a book for people who aren't on boards. In part, I am. Better than anything before it, this book will help the average person grasp what legitimate board work is about. It's ideal for the middle manager who wonders what the company's board is really for. It's important for the majority of investors who are brave enough to put some of their hard-earned savings into stocks but are too intimidated to attend an annual meeting. It's what all front-line volunteers in a community service group need so they understand the part the board has to play.

But even more, *The Imperfect Board Member* is a book for actual board members. The author—a friend of mine—often jokes that a greeter at Wal-Mart gets more orientation than most board members ever do. We all know that's no joke. It's true for boards of every description. And it's appalling. Although it sounds extreme, management guru Peter Drucker wrote, "There is one thing all boards have in common . . . They do not function."

For over a decade, Jim Brown and his team have been helping boards overcome their dysfunctions and govern well. Now this book extends the clarity of their perspective and the wisdom of their insights to everyone who cares enough to make a difference.

Jim does all this by painting a picture of real, likeable people struggling to be better board members and leaders. As they encounter twists and turns and pitfalls, we learn and grow with them. Whether we're directors of large corporations or board members of small community non-profits, we see ourselves in this story. Most important of all, we're left with a renewed vision. Boards really can add value to the organizations they serve. Board members really can work together in meaningful and rewarding ways. And even though we all have imperfections, governance excellence really is possible.

July 2006   PATRICK LENCIONI

BOARDS MATTER

.W. hen my partners and I began our consulting practice in the middle of the 1990s, most people had no idea what the word *governance* even meant. Typically, board members presumed they were elected or appointed because of their wisdom and experience. Typically, CEOs and executive directors considered the board to be a necessary nuisance. Neither board members nor senior executives considered board coaching or director development to be of consequence. Indeed, there seemed to be a stigma that accepting any such service would be tantamount to admitting they were not qualified to be at the board table.

So much has changed in just over a decade! As devastating as the debacles at Enron and WorldCom have been, those disasters and others like them have catalyzed a fundamental shift in how people view boards and their role. As Ram Charan told me with relief, "Thanks to Sarbanes-Oxley, boards have become active." Charan refers, of course, to the Sarbanes-Oxley Public Company Accounting Reform and Investor Protection Act of 2002. In Charan's terminology, explained for all of us in his excellent book, *Boards That Deliver,* boards are evolving from being "ceremonial" to "liberated" and ultimately to "progressive."[1] What Ram observes and describes is a process—a journey toward governance excellence.

Imperfect Board Members

No one wants to be known as "the imperfect board member." But we board members are all imperfect, because no one is flawless and no one knows everything. Fortunately, this need not prevent us from having a great board, as the best boards are teams of highly talented and experienced people who bring unique strengths and complement each other's weaknesses.

There is so much we need board members to bring to the table. Understanding the complexities of Sarbanes-Oxley and related legislation is important. Being able to interpret the organization's financial reports expertly is crucial. Having the ability to detect and examine emerging trends in our sector and then strategically anticipate opportunities and impacts is powerful. These all exemplify what my colleagues and I say makes a board "smart."

Smart and Healthy

As critical as it is for boards to be smart, this is what economists call necessary but not sufficient. Bill Dimma, a distinguished veteran of governance with experience on fifty-five corporate boards and almost as many non-profits, has diagnosed what he calls "the classic board dilemma." In his marvelous book, *Tougher Boards for Tougher Times*, Bill reminds us that right up to the time of their demise, the boards of Enron and Nortel were composed of people with outstanding talent and credentials.[2] He judges it as a case of individual competence and collective incompetence.

It is obvious that having the skills and knowledge to perform as a smart board is not enough. It is also imperative that boards be *healthy*. By this, we refer to issues including the level of trust and candor that exists at the board, the clarity of the respective roles of board and management, the relationship dynamics within the board, and the determination of the directors to subordinate their personal interests and serve the interests of the shareholders or members.

This concept of "smart and healthy" was introduced to us by my friend Patrick Lencioni and his team at The Table Group.

They observe that successful organizations share both quali-
ties.[3] He agrees with us that the principle applies profoundly
to boards as well. So our consulting and coaching practice is
fueled by a passion to help board leaders understand their
role and fulfill it with confidence and excellence. We are convinced that this is only possible when boards become *both*
smart and healthy.

In the growing section on bookstore shelves for governance,
some books are superb. Many are not. Regardless, the vast
majority of them focus on improving the smartness quotient
but ignore the healthy dimension. This book places greater
emphasis on the healthy side, while laying a foundation for
both aspects. It is not, however, a recipe for board work.
There are specifics and complexities beyond the scope of
this book, many best addressed by a professional familiar
with your particular situation.

A Quick Read, A Fun Story

This book is especially written for the millions—and there
are tens of millions of directors of non-profit and for-profit
organizations in North America alone—who are serious about
their board service but already swamped with the demands
of their other work, family, and community commitments.
I have deliberately made this book short enough that you
could read it on a flight from New York to Denver or in a

single evening. (Please don't try to read it during a board meeting, no matter how tempting!)

The journey toward governance excellence is a process of discovery. With inspiration and coaching from renowned authors Ken Blanchard and Patrick Lencioni, *The Imperfect Board Member* has been crafted to convey this journey in a style that allows you to travel the road as an interested observer. Perhaps you will even find yourself identifying with the characters. They are fictional, but they are representative and composite of so many leaders with whom I have had the privilege—and challenge—of working.

Discipline for Directors

As the story unfolds, you will see the characters discover the seven disciplines of governance excellence. These disciplines apply to all boards, and this story traces the journeys of both a corporate board and a non-profit board learning and practicing the disciplines in their settings.

Discipline, as we use it here, is something we *do* methodically, deliberately, and adeptly. It also refers to how we train to improve strength and control. Although some associate discipline with pain or even oppression, that need not be the case. In the context of sports, academics, and personal health, having discipline is generally understood to lead to desired results. I trust you are reading this book because you desire to see results from the boards you are on or work with.

More Than a Story—Prepare to Take Action

To help you apply the principles and practices presented in the story, a section at the end of the book reviews the model, offers tools and tips, and lists resources. All of this can help you no matter what your connection to a board—as a seasoned director, a beleaguered executive, an interested stakeholder, or a hopeful future board member. I sincerely hope you gain insights and understanding and take your next step to a healthy board.

A valuable resource for my own understanding of governance—and that of countless others—has been the innovative and thoughtful work of John Carver. He is a pioneering leader in this field. His seminal book, *Boards That Make a Difference*,[4] has provoked board leaders around the world to think deeply and differently about board work. For over twenty years, he has been articulating and expounding his Policy Governance® model, boldly and accurately endorsed by Sir Adrian Cadbury as "a significant advance in management thinking, as near a universal theory of governance as we at present have."[5]

Guelph, Ontario   JIM BROWN

THE
IMPERFECT
BOARD
MEMBER

CHAPTER ONE

ON THE EDGE

.**D**. avid lay in a cold sweat, heart pounding, staring wide-eyed at the ceiling. With a shaking hand he reached for his wife, Nancy. Relief flooded through him as he felt her warm back. Slowly, he scanned the darkened room. He was home. He was all right. It was just a dream.

He was six for six. Six nights, six nightmares. And always the same. A failed company. Disgrace in his profession. Loss of his house. Abandoned by his wife and son. His whole world torn apart.

He was angry with himself for not being able to get back to sleep. And he knew that the longer he was angry, the longer it would take to get back to sleep. The worst part was that he had no reason to believe that the next night would be any better.

In silent anguish, his thoughts went back to when he first began exploring the idea of taking his company public. He had been excited—even exhilarated—at the prospect. Friends at the country club teased him when he casually mentioned the possibility of an IPO. "Oh," they let loose, "you're signing up for one of those 'Instant Prosperity Options,' are you?" He laughed with them, but secretly he expected that their play on words was appropriate. Now, with the initial public offering behind him, he would change those words to "Impending Pressure Overload."

David could stand it no longer. He was now so awake, he listened for every sound. Slowly, he rolled out of bed and fumbled toward the bathroom. He flicked on the light, squinting in the unforgiving glare, and reached for the glass. Catching his reflection in the mirror, he wondered, *Who is this man?* For years he had been told he defied his age. In fact, he had almost rejoiced when his temples finally grayed. He wanted to be taken seriously—he needed to be considered a real contender in his industry.

Now, rubbing his stubbled jaw, David saw dull gray eyes and hollow cheeks. He noticed his T-shirt was tight across the middle. Too many meals on the run and late at night. It appeared that he had aged eight years in the eight months since the initial public offering.

He leaned on the counter. "What have I done?" he whispered and closed his eyes. *Everything I care about is on the line. Everything!*

He pulled his robe from the back of the door and flipped off the light. If he dealt with his e-mail, that would be one less thing to do at the office, he figured, so he headed downstairs to the study.

◆ ◆

"As our annual meeting comes to a close, I think I speak for everyone when I say . . ." The chairman's words faded out as David's mind was inundated with other thoughts. Feeling some obligation to show interest in his community, he had attended a meeting of a neighborhood association. Never one to squelch his own opinion, he had made several comments during the proceedings. *What have I done?* he complained to himself. *The last thing I need is another commitment. And for a community group? They're probably so disorganized I'll hate every minute. I already hate every minute. And I hate the thought of telling Nancy—she will hit the roof . . . No, she'll probably just roll her eyes and walk away with that classic victim look on her face. Maybe I shouldn't tell her . . .*

"Congratulations!" The word startled David out of his whirl-pool of inner whining. He snapped on his positive, profes-sional countenance—the one he had mastered after his MBA course on public relations, in which he learned to "always be sincere, even if you have to fake it." Turning, he saw it was a fellow director.

"Oh, thank you. Same to you—Trevor, isn't it?" With a nod of confirmation from Trevor, David went on, "It looks like

you and I will be the newcomers to the board for this year."
David wanted to tell him that they were probably both going
to regret this day, but his diplomacy prevailed. "I believe that
people have to give back to their community if they expect
community to really exist. I've always been interested in the
role that Cedar Grove Community Care has had in the area.
I'm hoping to learn more and help make great things happen."

Surveying his companion, David observed that Trevor was
tall and slim, wearing blue trousers and a mock turtleneck.
Although more casual for an official meeting of this sort
than David would be comfortable wearing, it was not incon-
gruent with the attire of many others. His gunmetal gray hair
was cropped short. His smile was welcoming; his eyes, a
sparkling blue.

There was something about Trevor that David found compelling. Perhaps it was his intensity. He seemed to listen with
great interest. When he had spoken earlier in the meeting, he
appeared to exude passion regarding the issues. Or maybe
he had just done a better job of internalizing the public relations lessons.

"It's wonderful to hear someone talk the way I think," said
Trevor. David chuckled to himself, thinking Trevor probably
had no idea how accurately he had phrased that sentence—it
really was just "talk" that David had offered! "Cedar Grove
Community Care is a remarkable organization," continued

Trevor. "I don't actually know of another instance where a city has relinquished the parks and recreational facilities in an area to a citizens' group. What a fabulous arrangement to allow people in the community to direct services for themselves."

The air of passion and sincerity that Trevor projected was striking to David.

"It sounds like you're just the kind of person this board needs, David. Your involvement here tonight and your interest in giving back to your community are commendable. And it seems you have a lot of business experience that will be a real asset for the board."

"Well, Trevor, as CEO of CommuniTrek, I've learned a thing or two about leading organizations."

"That's great. As we *direct* and *protect* together with the other board members, we'll see some great things happen."

David smiled politely and was about to walk away when he caught himself. "What did you say? It sounded like some catch phrase from the police force."

"Oh, no," Trevor laughed. "I said 'direct and protect.' It's something I learned a while ago about being a board member. The job of a board is to direct and protect. It helps me be clear about what I just signed up for."

"I like that," David replied. "Thanks for sharing it." After Trevor said goodbye, David watched as he moved into the crowd, connecting genuinely with others. Turning to leave, David pulled out his BlackBerry. "Very interesting," he muttered as he recorded the nugget he had just learned.

David knew he should have gone home right after the Cedar Grove meeting, but he went to his office instead. He plodded through some paperwork on his desk and read some periodicals that had been waiting for attention for a couple of months. It was an uncomfortable moment when David realized that he was putting in time. He had to admit to himself he just was not looking forward to going home, but he should not put it off any longer. Besides, Nancy would probably be asleep by the time he got there.

It was well past midnight when David stepped out of his prized titanium silver Z4 Roadster. He waited until the garage door closed before he opened the door to the kitchen, hoping to ensure no one would be wakened. His heart sank when he saw the light shining from the den.

"David?" Nancy's voice was strained. He edged into her view.

"I went back to the office. Sorry, I'm later than I thought." He wondered how many times Nancy had heard those words.

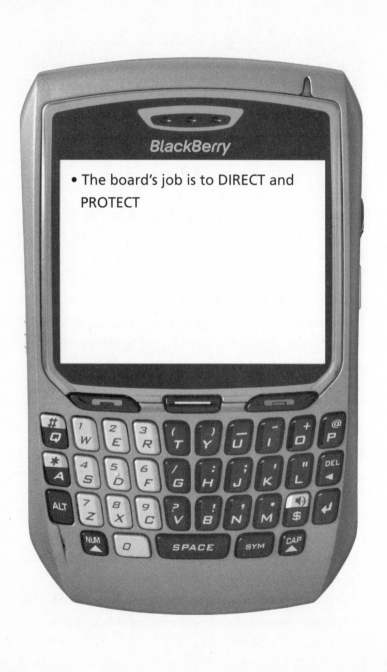

"We have a problem with Simon," Nancy blurted out. Her eyes looked bloodshot from crying.

David's immediate reaction was an internal sigh, thinking, *Oh great. Like I need another problem to try and solve.* Then he shook himself and asked Nancy what was happening.

"He sauntered in about forty-five minutes ago. He wouldn't tell me where he'd been or why he was late. He's only thirteen! It's a school night. He's not getting enough sleep. And he certainly isn't doing enough homework! I don't trust his friends." The words tumbled from Nancy as she paced the room.

"I just don't understand that boy," said David. "He never listens to me. I've told him a thousand times to be home by ten on school nights!"

"Maybe that's the problem," Nancy shot back. David looked confused. "You say you don't understand him because he never listens to you. But you'll never understand him unless you start listening to *him*.[1] Simon wants a Dad, but you never seem to have time for him."

"Oh Nancy. Let's not get into this. We both need some sleep. I have an early start tomorrow. I'm going to bed."

"See, that's what I mean. You don't have time for family. Go ahead, go to bed. I'm too upset to sleep. I'm staying here."

David turned to the stairs, feeling a mix of anger and guilt. And fatigue and fear—it was nighttime again.

The next day in the office started like most others. David arrived early, well before the crowd, but found a few other people already on the job. There was something comforting to him about seeing employees working even earlier than he started. It gave him a reason to believe some of his people had a work ethic that could carry the business where he wanted it to go.

He was convinced that hard work was central to the success his company had earned. Since the early days, he had doggedly driven sales, determined to build the company on revenue, not just potential. CommuniTrek more than doubled its revenues for four consecutive years. Although that growth rate had not been sustained, he had seen revenue catapult from $20 million to $90 million in the past three years. But he felt a desperate need to attract hard workers to the company for it to grow as planned.

He was quickly into the thick of things. Immersed in reports. Developing projections. Examining opportunities. However, it seemed that little had been accomplished by the time the first knock came on his open door. His marketing manager was concerned about how production delays would impact customers' expectations given the advertising that had already begun. And then it continued, from putting out one fire to dealing with the next.

David sometimes wondered if he would get anything done in a day if he did not start early and stay late. There were just so many distractions. Not that they were fruitless demands on his time, but the concern was that it just did not allow him enough time to focus on the big picture—growing the business. Then he had to go home to flaring emotions, teenage hormones, and chores—more distractions.

Mid-afternoon, he uttered an audible groan. Raising both hands to his forehead, he asked himself, "What good is my board?" For the fourth time in one day, he had encountered a problem that he traced back to another ball dropped by a director.

In preparation for listing the company, they had made some changes to the board. They had added a couple of higher-profile names, addressed what he was told was an "international void," and included a stronger finance person. The experts assured him that these changes were critical to garner investor confidence about the board's ability to govern the organization. This increased the number of directors from five to nine, including himself as chairman, and almost tripled what was being paid for board work.

Some boards seem to be a necessary nuisance—the system requires them but they add no value.

At first he was optimistic that the changes would be justified, but each month he found the situation more lamentable. Basically, the board seemed to be a necessary nuisance—the system required it but he felt it added no value. Muwanga was the much-hailed Ugandan diplomat who had political and business contacts in over a dozen African countries. Big deal. Six months had gone by and he had not opened a single door for sales on that continent. The two "high-profile" people had done nothing. Apparently they were so important they could not find time to come to the board meetings. And if the finance whiz was so bright, why had he required so much time from the management team? Hollingsworth, a long-time friend and member of the board from the early days, was a great guy, but why was he doing nothing to help get these new directors into the game?

Suddenly his thoughts went to his own new directorship with Cedar Grove. He realized that he had been sidetracked several times during the day with the memory of the meeting last night and his talk with Trevor. There was something about him . . . a depth of wisdom, perhaps. *I wonder if he's had to deal with his world unwinding around him,* mused David.

The phone on his desk startled him back to the present. He answered. To his surprise and satisfaction, it was Trevor.

CHAPTER TWO

A GLIMMER

OF HOPE

.**A.** t Trevor's suggestion, David agreed to an early morning get-together at a Coffee Pub. David pushed up the starting time, partly because he did not want a nonwork commitment to eat into his work day and partly because he wanted to see if Trevor was up to a meeting at six o'clock in the morning. He was surprised at the number of people in the place at that hour—it was nearly packed, yet there was only a subdued hum of voices and clinking of cups.

David saw Trevor motion to him from a booth across the room. "Good morning," David said, pleased that Trevor had risen to the challenge of an extra-early appointment. "You look bright and ready for the day," he added as he sat on the padded bench.

Trevor smiled. "I find that when I get an early start in the morning, I always feel better about the rest of my day."

Before they went any further, their attention was drawn to a man a couple of tables away who began complaining that his coffee was too slow in coming. The waitress snapped back some excuse and splashed some java into the man's cup.

"Your 'early-start' approach doesn't seem to work for them," David whispered to Trevor. "They're both up early but already going downhill." At that moment, the waitress wheeled around and strode toward him, coffee pot steaming and fully loaded. David sucked in a breath, fearful she had heard his wisecrack.

"Coffee to start?" she barked. David was speechless. He just pushed his cup and saucer toward her, not wanting to look in her eyes but afraid to take his eyes off her. She seemed mad enough to pour the potful onto someone, and he did not want to be the target.

"I'd like a cup too, please," Trevor inserted with a penetrating smile. "And I wonder if you could bring me some change for a twenty—I'd like to give you a good tip today."[1]

David's head jolted from the waitress to Trevor, eyebrows raised.

"There's your coffee . . . and I'll be right back with some change, sir," said the waitress, her voice and countenance transforming in the span of the sentence. She turned with a skip and a smile.

"Whoa, aren't you the manipulative one?" David looked at Trevor with surprise.

"I'm just creating the environment for her to be her best. I view tips differently than many people do. I like to use them To Inspire Premium Service. Why wait until it's too late to give her a message about her performance?"

"That's quite a concept," David said, fascinated by this man in yet another way. Not only was Trevor intense and full of zest, but he also had some thoughtful and unconventional ways of looking at things. "Listen, I really don't have much time. But it may be helpful for us to get on the same wave-length as we start into this board work with Cedar Grove."

Trevor's blue eyes lit up. "This is going to be fun. I'm very optimistic that we could establish a model that gets repeated in lots of other communities."

"Gee, I appreciate your excitement." David leaned back in his seat, almost unable to cope with Trevor's energy. "But I don't mind telling you that I've had some second thoughts about how I can fit this into my overcrowded life. These non-profit boards are notorious for chewing up time and going nowhere. I'm afraid it's going to be terribly frustrating."

"Hmm. I understand your concern. There are lots of boards out there that may be more troublesome than helpful, non-profit and otherwise. But I don't expect that with Cedar Grove. I've heard promising reports that this board has a good handle on its role, and I think Cynthia, the executive director, is very competent and professional. The city's commitment to fund Cedar Grove as a pilot for the next five years means there shouldn't be any of the fundraising crises that can sometimes plague non-profits. Sure, as with any board, there'll be some frustrations, but I'm anticipating a fulfilling experience. Besides, I think the success of Cedar Grove will be a great advantage for our community."

David was disarmed by Trevor's confident, informed, and rational assessment of the situation. Maybe his board tenure would not be so bad after all. He might even enjoy some of it.

David brought his Z4 to rest at an angle, spanning two parking slots at the community center. Hastily, he proceeded to the room designated for the Cedar Grove Community Care board meeting. He had worked up to the last possible moment in his office, dreading the notion of arriving early and sitting idly to wait for other directors to show up. Goodness knows he had endured plenty of wasted time waiting for members of his own board to arrive. Traffic had delayed him more than he expected, so rather than arriving right on time, he was a few minutes behind schedule. He was shocked to open the meeting room door and discover everyone seated and the discussion under way.

Earlier, when he and Trevor were confirming the timing of this upcoming meeting, David had insinuated that he was not exactly eager to attend. "If you've seen one board meeting, you've seen 'em all," he had pronounced. Trevor had cautioned him about the danger of preconceptions, and he was already feeling like a victim of them.

He was greeted by Amanda, the new board chair. "Oh, David, please join us. We're just going around the room sharing one thing about ourselves that we expect no one here knows. This should be easy for you since you're new to all of us. I won't take time to have the people repeat what they've already said, but I'll ask our two remaining directors to share next so you have a minute to think."

From that moment, the meeting unfolded in a lively and energizing manner, methodically advancing through the entire agenda and wrapping up a few minutes ahead of the intended adjournment time. David found himself feeling a mixture of pleasure and disbelief. Having expected that the meeting would consume the entire evening, he had warned Nancy he would be late. With that sense of space, he was comfortable trying to fit in a short visit.

"Wanna grab a beer, Trevor? This gives us something to talk about."

"It'll be great to debrief for a bit, David. Let's go to the Coffee Pub. I'll follow in my car."

At the Pub, after each selecting a flavored coffee, they sat comfortably amidst the bustling crowd. "Well, Trevor, that was quite an experience. I have to admit, I feel awkward for being late. I couldn't believe so many people were there and already started. My only comfort is that one other person didn't even show up."

"Actually, Amanda shared at the outset that Curt Helier called her a few days ago to report that he would be unable to attend the meeting, but he'd forwarded his thoughts on some key agenda items by e-mail. I think you should tell the chair how you feel. Do you think you'll have trouble attending for the start times in the future?"

David felt like a puppy with his nose slapped. "No," he muttered, "and I already apologized to Amanda. I'm actually a bit obsessive about being on time for meetings, but I have an even stronger phobia about wasting time because a meeting doesn't start on schedule. I was expecting most people to be late. I'm horrified that it was me. And that I was the only one. Thank goodness Amanda started without me."

"Amanda showed some real strength in her role as chair," Trevor agreed. He leaned toward David as he continued. "I told you that Cedar Grove is not like a lot of other boards. What did you see that stood out tonight?"

David looked into Trevor's eyes as he began, "Well, let's come back to the point I just made. It's funny. As a chairman, I've always felt uncomfortable starting meetings before all the board members were present. But I just realized that as an individual member I feel more uncomfortable with the weight of everyone waiting for me. Because of my experience tonight, I'm going to begin my board meetings on time even if some of the others haven't shown up."

"Hey," said Trevor, "it sounds like you've already gained some value from your volunteering!"

David smiled. "And that's not the half of it. Another thing I appreciated about the meeting was that Amanda simply kept things moving. She excelled in seemingly little details. Like not taking time for people to repeat what was shared before I arrived. When I finished telling the group about myself, I wished I had heard what the other directors had said, but it was best for the board not to be penalized for my tardiness. After that, she was artful in drawing out people's thoughts and redirecting the flow of input when others began to repeat points or seemed to be speaking for the sake of saying something.

"I have to admit, I've never been to a regular board meeting where everyone was asked to stand up for a couple of minutes with someone from the other side of the table to identify pros and cons on a proposal. I was surprised how much energy was built and how thorough the list became in that short time."

Trevor jumped in. "I agree. Adding some creativity to the process injected new life just when people were beginning to wane. What a pity that so many board meetings become *boring* meetings because everyone seems predisposed to sit in their seats and just talk. You can be sure that I'll use Amanda's technique sometime in the future."

"So will I. In fact, I can take advantage of a number of ideas from this meeting." David paused and then raised a finger toward Trevor. "Here's a question for you, though. When we spoke at the annual meeting, you shared a nugget that has been coming back to my mind repeatedly. You said that 'a board's job is to direct and protect.'

Many board meetings become boring meetings
because everyone seems predisposed to
sit in their seats and just talk.

"I really liked that. But I'm wondering about it now, because I can't see how the little introduction exercise Amanda had us do at the start of the meeting is either directing or protecting.

Was she wrong to do it or is directing and protecting too simplistic?"

Trevor smiled, seemingly enjoying the fact that David was thinking so seriously about board work. "There's *what* a board is supposed to do and then there's *how* the board will do it. 'Direct and protect' certainly is a simple way to describe the board's role. But that doesn't mean it's easy to do the job. One of the keys for a board to be able to fulfill its role well is knowing the strengths and backgrounds of each person around the table. The time we spent learning a bit more about each other helps us put people's ideas into perspective. And the way that Amanda had us working in pairs to list our thoughts supports the same purpose. I call all this interaction 'connecting.'"

"That's neat. To direct and protect, the board must connect. This is really helpful." David stretched, taking in a deep breath. "I'm kind of surprised to say this, but I'm looking forward to the next Cedar Grove meeting."

"Me too!" replied Trevor, downing the final sip of his coffee. "But I'd better run now, or my family won't let me go to any more of these meetings." David had risen to shake Trevor's hand and bid him good night, planning to leave himself. However, his cup wasn't quite empty and his thoughts were overflowing. Eager to capture the insights from their evening, he pulled out his BlackBerry and keyed in some notes.

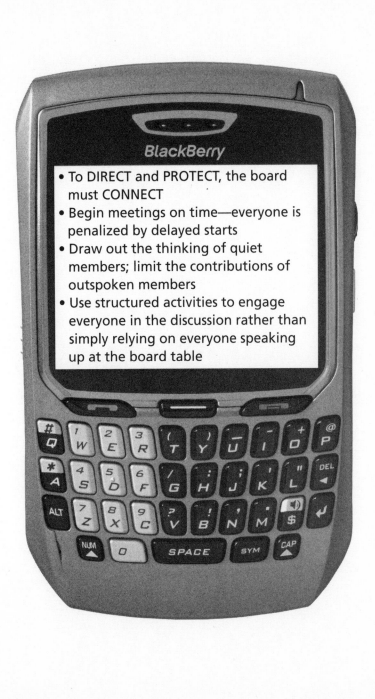

CHAPTER THREE

THE SECRET

FORMULA

$\blacklozenge$ L $\blacklozenge$ ife has a way of rushing by. The days quickly turned to weeks, and before David knew it, another Cedar Grove board meeting had come and gone. Between the two, he had managed to squeeze in a couple more helpful visits with Trevor. However, this second board meeting had left him frustrated. The group seemed to talk in circles about some concerns he had raised. He was particularly troubled with the fact that Trevor seemed to abandon him and his cause. Wanting to cut short the downward spiral of "what ifs" about his new friend, he picked up the phone.

Trevor answered his cellular. "Oh hi, David . . . Sure we can talk. I'm going to be downtown this afternoon—should I drop by your office?" They agreed to see each other around three o'clock, and David returned his focus to the pressing matters at CommuniTrek.

$\blacklozenge$ $\blacklozenge$

David motioned for Trevor to come in and sit while he finished up a phone call. Trevor stood to shake hands as soon as David hung up. "What a great office you have, David. I've driven by the building before, but never been inside. I like it—it's well appointed, yet very functional. How do you enjoy it?"

"Oh, fine." David looked sideways for a moment. "It's funny really. For years I dreamed of an attractive office suite that would suit how I saw myself as a professional. I spent lots of time choosing the furnishings I wanted and the colors I liked. Now, I come to work, sit down, and get busy. I really don't think about it anymore. I feel almost foolish for allowing myself to get caught up in the details of my decorating while so many more important things were before me.

"Anyway, enough of that. I wanted to talk with you about Cedar Grove."

"Fire away," Trevor said with a smile.

"Well, I'm not exactly sure how to start. Part of me wants to ask if I did something to upset you and the other part of me wants to ask why you upset me."

"Wow. You've caught me by surprise on both counts," Trevor replied. "I'm not upset and I wonder why you think I might be. And I certainly have no idea about your being upset. Help me understand."

29

"Oh, it's just that at the meeting last week you seemed unwilling to support me. I felt like you had ditched me just when everyone was spinning their wheels on the issues I raised." David was relieved he had said it, but apprehensive about how Trevor might respond.

"I'm sorry it looked that way to you, David. Let me assure you that I am always going to be your supporter." David unclenched his jaw at Trevor's words. "Sometimes the best way for me to support you will be for me to disagree." Now David drew his eyebrows together. "One of the 'issues' you raised that evening was that nighttime security patrols of the parks ought to be considered. What made you bring that up?"

"Well, it would be a service to the residents, increasing the safety in the area," David asserted.

"And had the staff received any such request, do you think?"

"Absolutely. I had suggested it to Cynthia myself a few weeks ago and as far as I can see, nothing's been done."

Trevor leaned toward David. "This is a problem, friend. You've changed hats. You're talking as a *customer* and expecting to be heard as an *owner*. You have a desire for service in your neighborhood. And you've shared enough with me about your son, Simon, that I'm guessing you might be hoping a night patrol could help guard against him getting mixed up in trouble when he's out later than you wish."

David shrugged, as if to say "So?"

"When we go to a board meeting, we go as directors, serving the organization on behalf of the owners."

"Yeah, and the owners are the people in the neighborhood. And I'm one of them," David rebutted.

"Let's back up and look at this differently. Think about CommuniTrek. Who are the owners? Sure, the shareholders are the owners. And who are the customers?"

Problems arise when board members talk as customers and expect to be heard as owners.

"Well, we have lots of different customers," David explained. "The big ones are governments and companies from all around the world. And then we have the thousands of individual users of our systems."

"Great. And what do you think would happen if one of them came into a board meeting of yours and started to ask for better service or complained about your products?"

"I'm sure you know they would never get through the door. The board doesn't have time to hear every individual customer's concerns," David replied.

"And does that mean that their concerns are trivial?"

"Definitely not. The moment CommuniTrek stops listening to its customers, we're on our way out of business. I've created a strong culture of customer service in my company."

Trevor stood and moved toward the whiteboard on the office wall. "I'm guessing that the customers are served by your staff. And that's how it should be. The secret to organizational effectiveness is understanding the different roles within an organization and how those roles relate."

The secret to effectiveness is understanding the different roles within an organization and how those roles relate.

He drew a diagram on the board with a large, flat oval on top, a similar-sized flat rectangle on the bottom, and a large triangle joining the two shapes. He wrote "Customers" in the bottom box. "In any organization, there must be someone being served—we'll consider them customers, though they actually may not be spending money. They may simply be 'recipients of services.'"

"The customers are served by staff," Trevor added as he printed that word in the triangle above "Customers." "And the CEO role is to be the point person for all of the staff." He wrote "CEO" at the point of the staff triangle and drew a line under it, making the top section a small triangle within the larger one.

"Now we come to the top of the diagram. The big oval represents all the owners," he explained, recording that label as well. "And from among the owners, a small group of people is selected to be the board." Trevor drew a small oval within the larger one so that it just touched the tip of the CEO triangle. "Since the board's job of directing and protecting is to be done on behalf of owners and in their best interest, it's best if the board is made up of owners.[1]

"It's important to understand that this is not so much an organizational chart as it is a map," Trevor went on. "It clarifies

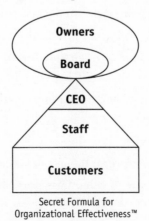

Secret Formula for
Organizational Effectiveness™

See endnote #1 for Chapter Three.

the roles within the organization and the relationships between those roles." He wrote "Roles & Relationships" at the top of the diagram. "I've learned to call this the 'Secret Formula for Organizational Effectiveness.' When it was explained to me, I was told that it wasn't intended to be a secret, but it must be, because most organizations have it so mixed up.

"When you think about these roles and how they relate, it helps to ask certain questions, like 'what will communication look like in this picture?' Organizational communication will follow a single straight line," Trevor said as he drew a line from the top of the diagram to the bottom, right through the tip of the triangle. He was clearly in "teacher" mode and David's curiosity was building, so he rose to stand at the board with Trevor. "Owners speak to the board. The board speaks—with a unified message, or one voice—to the CEO.[2] The CEO speaks to staff. And the staff speaks to the customers." Trevor put an arrow on the bottom of the line, indicating the direction of communication flow. "But communication follows the same straight line in the other direction—customers speak to staff, staff to CEO, CEO to board, and board to owners," he said, adding an arrowhead to the top of the line as well.

"Let's test this by looking at the implications of neglecting the single straight line. If customers stop talking to staff and come to you, the CEO, with all their concerns, what happens?"

"Chaos," David answered quickly. "I get bogged down with details and I'm unable to do my real job."

The Secret Formula is not an organizational chart; it is a map to clarify the roles and relationships within an effective organization.

"Exactly. But lots of customers would like the ear of the CEO. And some CEOs like spending lots of time with customers. Certainly they should spend *some* time with customers, but if they were objective and looked at themselves, they would feel the same discomfort you admitted feeling when you realized how much time you spent picking furniture and color schemes for your office. These are legitimate things to do, but the CEO is not the person to do them." The validity of this point resonated with a sting for David.

"Now, what are some implications of CEOs not talking to their staff, but always talking directly with customers?"

David was rapid in his reply. "Again, their time will be consumed in lower-payoff activities. But there'll also be a

Roles and Relationships

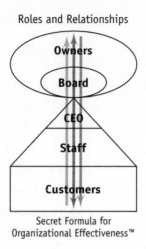

Secret Formula for
Organizational Effectiveness™

detrimental impact on the staff. They're going to be asking themselves why they're even on the job if the CEO is doing all the customer contact. They're going to feel unappreciated, maybe even mistrusted. The good staff members will eventually leave and find a job that's more fulfilling."

"This is why you get the big bucks—you're a quick study!" Trevor said and smiled. "How about the implications of board members bypassing the CEO and talking directly to staff?"

"Well, that's the same thing at a different level. The CEO is going to feel out of the loop, maybe even usurped. And the staff may be confused about who they ought to listen to—the board members or the CEO. I can tell you, I'd be looking for a way to get that board member out of the picture, because if he's left unchecked, it's only a matter of time before the CEO will be pushed out of the picture."

When the single straight lines of communication, authority, and accountability get broken, confusion and chaos result.

Trevor enjoyed David's speedy insights. "The same kinds of problems occur wherever the single straight line of communication gets breached. You used the word 'chaos,' and I think that describes it well. Remember, though, what we're talking about is official communication between roles. I'm not for a moment saying it's wrong for any person at any place in the organization to simply talk to another person."

Trevor picked up a different color of marker and drew another line, essentially on top of the earlier one, down through the middle of the diagram. "Another dimension to examine is authority. In effective organizations, authority follows a single straight line. The owners have authority over the board. The board has authority over the CEO. The CEO has authority over the staff. And the staff has authority over customers— at least in some ways." Trevor added an arrowhead to the bottom of the line. "Authority flows in one direction only.

"Similarly, accountability follows a single straight line." Trevor drew yet another line in another color on top of the other two. "But this one flows in the opposite direction. The customer is accountable to the staff, if only to pay for things before he walks out of the store. More obviously, the staff is accountable to the CEO. The CEO is accountable to the board. And the board is accountable to the ownership."

David jumped in. "I can see the same kind of chaotic repercussions arise when the straight lines of authority or accountability get broken. People are confused about who to listen to. A culture of covering your back gets built. It becomes a nightmare."

"Well, David, you've been very patient to work through this with me as I try to explain my concern about the board discussion last week. Do you see now why it's so dangerous for board members in a board meeting to raise customer concerns, not ownership issues? It becomes a slippery slope toward distraction from the legitimate board discussion, confusion between the people involved, and chaos in the organization.

"You can certainly talk to the staff about your customer concerns, emphasizing that you're speaking as a resident, not a board member. But that's you, David, in a different role—the customer role—relating to the appropriate connection point in the Secret Formula—the staff."

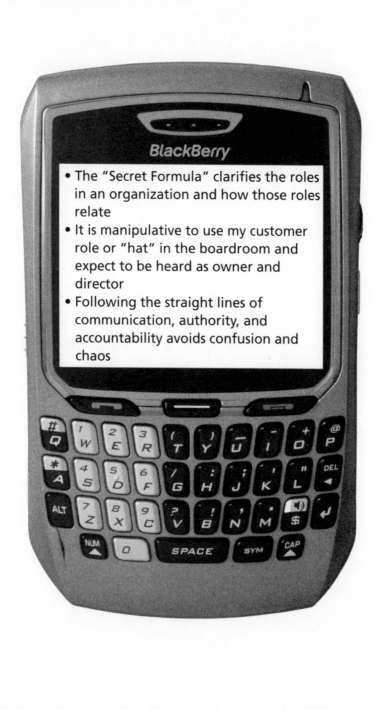

David digested the words. "I can see what you're saying. It seemed innocent, even appropriate, at the meeting. But there is a downside I wasn't even imagining.

"I think I'm grasping the Secret Formula in general, but I'm still having some trouble seeing how it fits some specific situations."

"Well, we'll talk more. But I need to run, and you have lots to do." Trevor slapped David's shoulder and departed.

David did need to turn his attention back to CommuniTrek, but he was determined to make some notes of what he had learned from Trevor before moving on. Pulling out his Black-Berry, he jotted down some thoughts. Then, because "a picture is worth a thousand words," he used a graphics program on his computer to create a sketch of the diagram and forwarded it to his handheld.

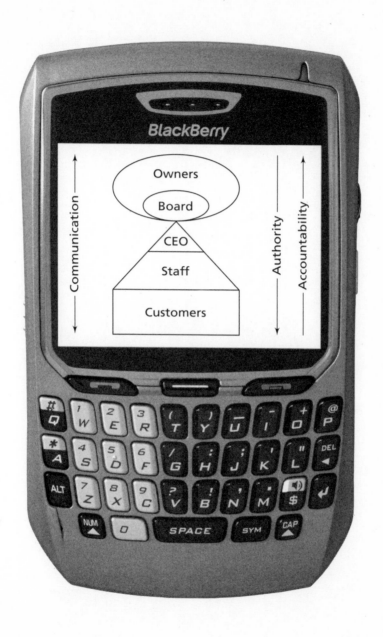

CHAPTER FOUR

THE ENEMY

WITHIN

．D． avid rolled his eyes as he picked up the phone. A moment before, his assistant, April, had poked her head through his doorway to tell him—almost apologetically—that Ron Eckstein was holding on line five for him.

"Hi, Ron. How can I help you today?" David began with forced friendliness. Then he mostly listened while the board member unloaded a barrage of thoughts and demands. There were figures Ron wanted explained. There were reports he believed the board ought to be getting. There were concerns about a recent print advertising campaign.

David responded to the concerns as well as possible and politely concluded the call with "We'll see what we can do to address these items and get back to you, Ron."

Most everything inside him had wanted to scream "Buzz off and let me do my job!" Eckstein's meddling was both a bother and a burden. Too much of David's time—and the time of people on his management team—was siphoned off by demands from this board member. And the nature of the

44

demands was beginning to get under David's skin. It almost seemed that Eckstein was on a mission to discredit him.

David realized he was under considerable pressure, so he pushed back those fears, determined to prevent paranoia from gripping him. But regardless of the motives, how could Eckstein's meddling be justified? Old Hollingsworth would never be so intrusive. On the other hand, Eckstein had been on a couple of corporate boards—a credential lacking in both Hollingsworth and himself. David felt the interference and inefficiency caused by Eckstein's involvement was an imposition. Still, he was conscious that he might be guilty of interfering somewhat himself.

He had learned how to get what he wanted from his previous board. Most issues just needed to be explained in the "proper" light. As successful as most of the previous directors had been in their fields, they certainly did not understand CommuniTrek or the communication business like he did. Offering just the right amount of technical jargon and market data could shift the group into "nodding" mode. David could easily recognize when people began agreeing with things when they did not really understand them. He surmised that the directors had been quite confident in his ability and did not want to risk asking any "stupid questions" that would reflect poorly on themselves. For decisions that might be more contentious, he had learned that it was easier to get forgiveness than permission. He would simply do what he and the management team had decided was best and take the flak at the board meeting when he reported it. Things got uncomfortable at times, but none of the decisions ended up being reversed. "Water under the bridge" was the metaphor that prevailed.

All of this worked for him. His methods were certainly expedient. His problem was the nagging discomfort he felt because of a connection this had to a conversation with his son the night before.

"Oh, Dad. I see what you mean. Sorry. But it's too late now— I've already ordered it on eBay." In that instant, David had restrained his natural reaction because his psyche was still smarting from the accusations Nancy had made several weeks earlier. He really did want to understand his son, and he knew that yelling at him would not improve the relationship. Not knowing what else to do, he had just turned and walked away silently, knowing that this was not a long-term solution either.

With these thoughts rumbling in his mind, he picked up the phone almost instinctively and called Trevor's cell number. As it was ringing, he wondered what he was going to say. He would have hung up, but he knew that his number would show up on Trevor's phone and only create awkward questions later.

Hearing Trevor's ever-pleasant greeting, David began uncomfortably. "Trevor. I don't really know why I called, but it would be good if we could meet. This time I'll come to you. Where do you work, anyway?" David realized in that moment that Trevor's vocation had never come up in their conversations. He felt uneasy because they had certainly talked lots about CommuniTrek.

"I'm on the west end of Bank Street."

"That's only a few blocks from my house. I don't remember any office buildings in that area."

"I'm at Southridge Community Church. I'm a pastor here," Trevor explained.

There was silence . . . "Ah, gee Trevor. I never would have guessed. Why didn't you tell me?"

"It never really came up. I do admit, David, that I'm sometimes reserved about this because I find people often jump to strange conclusions about me when they learn about my work. But I really think in our case it was more that it never came up."

David was trying to reconcile conflicting images in his mind. He was about to say, "Aren't you guys supposed to wear white collars or something?" but he was certain this was the kind of strange conclusion that Trevor disliked. "I don't know what to think," he forced out. "But, you know what, that probably makes it all the more appropriate for me to talk with you. When can you see me?"

As David drove into the entrance at Southridge Community Church, he was unsure of what to expect. To his surprise, the older building close to the road connected to a huge, newer section behind it. The tree-shrouded front gave the impression that the property was much smaller. He parked in a large paved lot and followed signs easily directing him to the offices.

A polite woman welcomed him and asked how she could help. When she learned that he was looking for Trevor, her reply made it clear that she expected him. He was shown to a sitting area, informed that Trevor would be with him shortly, and offered a refreshment.

While sipping a fruit drink, he took inventory of all that he saw. Sunlight sprinkled the room through the maple trees outside the windows. A few small round tables were surrounded by comfortable, firm chairs. Magazines were fanned out neatly on a side counter that was topped by inset bookshelves. Tastefully framed posters and prints hung on the walls. He sat and looked toward the reception area where three people were busy at well-equipped workstations.

"Hi, David," Trevor greeted him as he strode into view. "Sorry to keep you waiting."

"It's only been a few minutes. I appreciate you making time for me on such short notice." On Trevor's lead, they walked into a neat office. "I've noticed the church sign off the street before but never really paid attention to the property. Your building goes on and on back there. And what's with all the cars in the parking lot? Isn't Sunday the day for action?"

"Oh, goodness, there's action here every day. We have an elementary school and there are always lots of other group activities under way. But you're right, the busiest days are on the weekends."

"Well, like I said, Trevor, I'm grateful you made time for me. Last night I had another aggravating time with Simon. I was hoping I could talk to you about it."

With Trevor's instant invitation, David recounted the details, explaining that Simon had charged his mother's credit card. "I could've killed him," David emphasized.

Trevor could tell David was not at all serious about that statement. "President Lincoln wisely judged that 'it never does a boy much good to shoot him.'"[1]

With a little chuckle, David went on to admit he felt like a failure for not responding appropriately. "I really don't know what to do. Am I a hopeless case, Doc?"

Trevor smiled. "Hope is a choice. Add to it perseverance and that's what changes the world.

Hope is a choice. Add to it perseverance
and that's what changes the world.

"Help me understand the situation more by answering some questions." At a nod from David, he continued, "Would you ever have spent as much on Simon as he charged for himself?"

"Sure. We're very fortunate, so we've been very generous with Simon. Spending $500 on a gift for him is not that unusual."

"OK. Would you ever have purchased for Simon what he ordered for himself?"

"I guess. Whether he really needs it is questionable, but there's nothing really wrong with him having it. The concern is how he got it. Without even asking, he used his mother's eBay account and incurred a sizable charge for a thirteen-year-old."

"Do you think he realized that this would be inappropriate?" Trevor probed further.

"I think he realized we wouldn't be pleased."

"Has he ever before done something he knew would be unacceptable?"

David's eyes opened wide. "Weekly," he said in a mechanical tone.

"And what happens?"

"Oh, I usually shout at him. Then Nancy gets quiet because she doesn't like me shouting. Then we all ignore it and it blows over."

"So, how's that working for you?"

David thought for a moment. "Did you get that question from Dr. Phil?"

Trevor had to smile.

"It definitely is not working," David confessed. "At least, it's not working for me. It's working very well for Simon, it seems."

"He's learned that it's easier to get forgiveness than permission," Trevor observed.

The color drained from David's face. "That's what's so scary. I think he learned that from me."

Trevor sat in silence. He had several thoughts he could have shared, but he realized that David needed to process further.

"That's what provoked my call this morning. I've realized that I work that way with my board. And I'm conscious that I hate it when Simon plays that game with me, so I'm wondering if the board feels the same way. And I'm thinking about the long-term effects of these lessons—bad lessons—that Simon has learned. And wondering if I've been deceiving myself by thinking there won't be negative impacts from my own practices in the long term."

"Wow. You *are* shining a light into some dark recesses." Trevor seemed pleased to see the level of self-awareness that David was demonstrating.

"I feel like 'I have met the enemy and the enemy is me.'"[2]

"Let's stay with Simon for the time being. What do you wish he had done?" Trevor asked.

"I'm so disappointed because somehow it seems that he thinks he can only get what he wants if he makes it happen for himself. The fact is, Nancy and I would do almost anything for him. We're on his side, not against him."

"So what do you wish he had done?" Trevor repeated.

"I wish he would just talk to us. Explain what he's thinking. Share his dreams. If he needs something, just ask us, for goodness sakes. We want the best for him." David stopped as a lump grew in his throat.

Sometimes we inadvertently reward the behavior we don't want and fail to reward the behavior we desire.

"A great little book called *The Greatest Management Principle in the World* [3] teaches the simple truth that 'what gets rewarded gets done.' This seems so basic, but it escapes us at times. The most penetrating aspect of the book for me was that it showed how often we inadvertently reward the behavior we don't want and fail to reward the behavior we desire.

"Could it be that you have unintentionally ignored or rejected his requests in the past?" Trevor knew his question was an uncomfortable one.

"Probably. Nancy's convinced that I don't listen to Simon—and considering how preoccupied I've been with work, it's likely true." David could tell where this was going.

"And you've already conceded that you tend to dismiss the times when he disobeys."

David closed his eyes slowly and nodded agreement.

"In other words, he gets what he wants when he disobeys."

Another nod.

"In other words, he gets rewarded for disobeying."

David turned and looked out the window. "Like I said, I feel like I'm failing and I don't know what to do."

Driving down winding rural highways with the Z4's top down always gave David a good feeling. And that is what he was looking for as he turned over in his mind the matters he

54

had discussed with Trevor. He could not shake the notion that his frustrations with Simon and with his board—particularly Eckstein—were more his fault than anyone else's. Trevor had asked some good questions. If only there were some answers.

CHAPTER FIVE

UNRAVELING

FROM THE

INSIDE

T he CommuniTrek board meeting adjourned abruptly and everyone filed out of the room without speaking. David made a beeline for his office and closed the door behind him, wanting to slam it but avoiding the attention.

It had been his intention to "come clean" during this meeting; to admit to the board that he had a tendency to push things forward and that he realized this might be dishonoring the board. But things had unfolded in a way he had never imagined.

Just as the meeting got under way, Eckstein started his familiar routine and it went downhill fast. Not only was he asking a lot of time-consuming questions, but he went from a tone of superiority to one of unquestionable accusation. Eckstein insinuated that David was filtering financial information and biasing the audit committee. The other board members were certainly taken aback, but none jumped to David's defense. When David attempted to explain that he had no opportunity to bias the audit committee, as he was not even a member, Eckstein insisted that he had plenty of influence. And then the worst happened. Eckstein quoted David. It was sorely out of context, but they were unmistakably his words. And the horrifying part was that there was no way Eckstein could have been present when David had uttered them.

"Maybe he has some bugging device installed in the office," David muttered to himself as he paced about his private office. But he knew this was ridiculous. The gut-wrenching reality was that there was only one reasonable explanation for how Eckstein had those words in his holster. Someone on the management team had told him. Someone had crossed the line.

When David's eyes opened, his office was spinning. *How could this happen?* he thought. Never in all his life had he fallen asleep at his desk during a work day. He turned to his computer and did a Google search on "medical signs of stress." He clicked on the first hit and groaned out loud as he read the prominent physical warning signs:

Dizziness or a general feeling of "being out of it"

Other items on the list only reinforced his self-diagnosis:

Problems sleeping
Headaches
Tiredness, exhaustion

"Good grief," he grunted, pushing his keyboard tray back under his desk. "As if I needed confirmation to know I'm under stress." He logged off of his computer, locked his desk drawers, and walked out of the office. April watched him depart, half trying to get his attention, but reluctant to disturb the cloud that seemed to surround him.

Another drive in the country in the Roadster cleared some turbulence from his mind. What a view! What an afternoon! What a car! A totally divergent thought came to his mind and he pulled the Z4 to the side of the road. Getting out his BlackBerry, he looked up a number and made a phone call. Now he was on a mission. He had about four hours to pull some things together in time for the evening meeting at Cedar Grove. It would require some computer work, so he decided to head back to the office. As awkward as it might be there, it would be less distracting than going home.

The moment the Cedar Grove board meeting concluded, David practically dragged Trevor to the parking lot. "Come on. Jump in my car—we'll get a coffee."

Trevor had not yet fastened his seat belt when David's furor began.

"Did you see what happened in there? I can't believe it. I spent hours developing the plan that I presented tonight, and a few blowhards who don't look like they did a blasted thing since our last meeting have the nerve to try to tear it apart. And Cynthia! Who does she think she is? Our lowly little executive director can't talk to me that way. I'm a board member. I could buy and sell her ten times over. I've got receptionists I pay more money than she makes. If I wasn't so new to the board, I would have given them all a piece of my mind."

David's emotions were high and climbing. Trevor was aware that they had just reached highway speed as they drove through the mall parking lot to reach the coffee shop.

"You were wise to restrain yourself," he said. He was thankful that David had not unleashed his emotions at the board meeting. "Say, David, let's use the drive-thru so we can sit and talk in your car—it's more comfortable than the seats in there." Although this was certainly true, his motive was to save David from making a scene in public.

"Good idea." David swerved in front of a car that was moving too slowly for him and accelerated into the drive-thru lane. Coming to an abrupt stop, he lowered his window and shouted their drink orders. "Trevor, I seriously doubted myself when I agreed to be on this board, and now I'm thinking it was a big mistake. I have a mind to resign tomorrow before this gets totally out of hand. Those people have no idea what demands I face. I feel like I've been totally wasting my time."

"You *are* very busy, David," Trevor acknowledged. "In fact, I'm amazed you found the time to put together that report you presented."

"Believe me, it came at quite a sacrifice," he shot back.

Without allowing him the time to continue, Trevor responded. "Maybe it was a wrong sacrifice."

"Yeah," replied David. "Wait a minute. What do you mean by that?"

"When I was a teenager, an uncle of mine moved back from across the country. He'd been totally out of contact with our family for years. Out of the blue, he called up and invited me to a major league ball game with him. I saw it as a gesture to build a bridge where there had been no real connection before, so I accepted."

David laughed. "Who wouldn't, Trevor? A free ticket to see the pros play America's pastime is an obvious choice!"

Raising his hand in a gesture that signaled "stop," Trevor rebutted him. "You're falling into the same trap he did. It turns out, I had a terrible time. I'd always found baseball ridiculously boring. An hour into that game, I was utterly convinced. I've never been to another baseball game since. But the worst part was how my uncle behaved. When he found out I wasn't familiar with the names of all the players, he said I must have grown up in a cave. When I didn't join him in jumping out of my seat and yelling vulgarities at the opposing team or the umpire, he told me I didn't know how to have fun. When he asked if I was having a good time, I thoughtlessly said something vague like 'I guess so' or 'pretty good.' With obvious aggravation, he shoved the ticket stubs in my face, pointing at the price, and complained that I was making him waste a lot of money on ball tickets, just sitting there like a bump on a log."

"Oooh. Sounds like there's a bit of pain from a past injury," David remarked. Turning to the window, he reached to receive the tray with two steaming cups, then handed Trevor his latté and secured his own before pulling away from the window.

"No, it's an ache from the fact that the scenario gets repeated so often in so many different ways. I know my uncle's intentions were good, but his assumptions nullified them. He made a sacrifice—which I now understand represented a lot of money in his situation—but it was a *wrong sacrifice*."

"There's that phrase—a wrong sacrifice. What are you getting at?" David nosed the Z4 into a parking spot well away from other cars.

"My uncle's financial sacrifice did him no good because he took something valuable to him—a bunch of his money—and gave something of low value to me—a baseball ticket. He assumed I would appreciate a trip to a ball game because he placed a high value on that, but that's an invalid assumption."

"Quite a story, friend," David admitted, "but I'm still missing the connection."

"You dug up some useful information about creating revenue streams through exclusive agreements with suppliers. However, you spent a lot of time exploring exactly how that could work and recommending that the board implement your plan. The board hadn't made that decision. It's a totally new direction. You hadn't been asked to do that work. And the board wasn't ready to go to that extent."

David tapped his hot cup with his fingers. "That's what makes this so hard to take. I bend over backwards to go the extra mile early in the journey with this board, and I get the opposite of thanks. I feel like I wasted my time."

"That's what I'm trying to tell you, David. You did waste your time, because you spent it on something that was of low value to the board. The work you did to gather some options was great, but all of the time you committed beyond that was unnecessary. When the board saw your recommendation, it was too new an idea with too little time for directors to digest the options. Besides, there weren't really options. You identified one option with potential and turned it into a plan. We all need to realize that a recommendation is a decision in disguise. And it's the board's job to make governing decisions, not a committee's, not an individual board member's."[1]

A recommendation is a decision in disguise.

"What do you mean? The board always has the option of approving the recommendation or not." David was thinking back to hundreds of recommendations that had come to CommuniTrek's board over the years.

"Absolutely. And this board turned it down. But your reaction shows that it wasn't really a recommendation in your mind. Just as most 'recommendations' are really more than that. They are *answers.*"

David was too charged to let this go easily. "If they would just trust me, we could move a lot faster and get a lot more done," he retorted. "What I presented is the right thing to do."

"David, you're a CEO. You're used to managing daily operations. Operations demand speed. In that setting, it's often better to make decisions knowing some will be wrong than to deliberate over issues and fail to act. But governance demands prudence. Directing and protecting well requires several people, not a lone ranger. Making time for the whole board to be properly informed and jointly convinced about a new direction is more appropriate than pushing forward, even if it does turn out to be the right thing to do."

Making time for the whole board to be properly informed and jointly convinced about a new direction is more appropriate than pushing forward.

"I can't swallow this. Getting recommendations is the routine way of working efficiently. We do it at our board meetings all the time. And I want it from my staff, too. I would be disgusted if one of my people brought me a report with options and no recommendation." David was animated in his defense.

Trevor grinned and said, "Sometimes a majority only means that all the fools are on the same side." Seeing only determined resistance in David's eyes, he continued more carefully. "David, there are times when things work well in one application and get transferred to another under the assumption that it will fit the new application, too. But that is faulty logic.

"When you're wearing your CEO hat, it makes sense to expect your staff to come to you with recommendations. This is a wise practice, because you're likely trying to develop their ability to make higher-level decisions. When you've seen enough evidence that a person repeatedly recommends answers that are optimal, you'll eventually let them make those decisions themselves so you are freed up for other responsibilities."

"Exactly," David agreed curtly. "And the more I can surround myself with competent decision makers, the more I can get done."

"Excellent. It's a great strategy for your application. But it doesn't apply to the board situation. If it's truly a board-level matter, the board must make the decision. Boards are not trying to train committees or individuals to make governing decisions on their behalf. That's an abdication of duty."

David blinked and managed a slight nod of acceptance on that point.

Trevor thought for a moment and then continued tentatively. "I'm not trying to pour fuel on the fire, so please think about this before reacting too strongly. When Simon ordered the electronic gadget on eBay, your frustration wasn't about the decision but the process. What happened tonight is the same thing. The Cedar Grove board may still choose to move in the direction you outlined. And Cynthia may choose to implement some or all of the plans that you presented. But the direction is the board's decision, not yours. And the board was not ready to make that decision, given the last-minute nature of the information it received. To insist that they approve your recommendation is to impose your will just as Simon did."

David sat glaring at Trevor, lips pursed, eyes steady. Seconds felt like minutes. Finally, he exhaled and turned away as he closed his eyes slowly.

"Trevor, my family life is a mess. My business is grinding me up. Today I thought I would put some extra energy into this stupid little volunteer activity to get a win under my belt, but now *everything* is in flames!"

They both sat quietly. Then Trevor spoke.

"When you're in the depths of despair, things appear dark in every direction. But when you raise your head out of the pit, you get a totally different perspective."

David responded without looking at Trevor. "Sometimes the walls of the pit are so slippery it feels like there is no getting out."

"Sometimes the best way out is for a friend to throw down a rope—but the person in the pit has to actually want to get out."

David turned to see Trevor's arm outstretched toward him. "Start pulling, pal," David said, reaching to clasp this hand of hope.

They talked for hours, dismantling false conceptions, considering alternative approaches, and formulating plans. Having regained some perspective, David asked to discuss the matter of recommendations further so he could make notes.

- Boards do not ask for or accept recommendations—a recommendation is a decision in disguise
- Boards DO ask people to bring options with pros and cons so they can make an informed decision
- Making time for the whole board to be properly informed and jointly convinced about a new direction is more appropriate than pushing forward

CHAPTER SIX

REBUILDING

FROM THE

GROUND UP

.I. want to apologize to all of you."

David's words caught the members of the management team somewhat by surprise. They had been summoned together on short notice and presumed that the agenda was some kind of emergency management.

"I've been feeling a lot of pressure recently and it has affected our work. I'm sorry about that."

The team members sat in silence, unsure of what to do. David's relationship with them had always been friendly, but very much professional.

"On top of pressures here at the office, I've been struggling with some things at home."

It was obvious that the others were wondering what was about to happen.

"I'm not making excuses. I'm just trying to let you in on the bigger picture. In fact, I'm conscious that I haven't really made space for that part of the picture in the office. I'm sorry about that, too. I doubt that I'll be able to make a fast change, but I want you all to know that I understand you have personal lives and they affect—and are affected by—your work."

Silence continued, with some glances of uncertainty among the people at the table. Finally Jerry, the chief operating officer, blurted out, "Wow. Does this mean we all have to hold hands and sing 'Kumbaya' now?"

Snorts turned to laughs, the loudest of all coming from David. "You guys are great!" he smiled. Jerry was renowned for bringing levity to any situation. His real name was Jerome, but everyone called him Jerry. The rumor was that it began because he was so much like Seinfeld, but most people figured he started that rumor himself. He had been one of the earlier hires that David made at CommuniTrek and, next to David, Jerry had the longest tenure of anyone on the management team.

"I'm not trying to be weird," David tried to reassure them. "I just want to be a better leader. Something I recently learned is 'The Secret Formula,' and it's helped me get a different look at our situation."

Again there were questioning looks, but a light mood prevailed. David went on to sketch out the Secret Formula and discuss the roles and relationships of the component players.

Then he guided a group discussion about the single straight lines of communication, authority, and accountability.

"You guys are sharp. And that's why I was so eager to share this with you. We've talked about the implications of any of those straight lines being violated. Let's go further, though." David had prepared for the next moment by planning to incorporate the meeting technique he had seen Amanda use. Handing out flip chart pages and markers, he instructed them, "Pair up and list on your flip chart three insights you see from the Secret Formula as it applies to us at Communi-Trek." While writing this instruction on the whiteboard, he told them he would allow three or four minutes for them to complete their lists.

A few minutes later, three pages were posted on the walls and the group was into an animated discussion about the application of the Secret Formula.

David had given this some prior thought, and he had a number of points he was wishing to discuss. To his amazement, most of them were listed. And the others had come up with some very valid points he had not even considered, some being a tad uncomfortable for him. He was careful not to deny or make excuses about concerns they raised. His grand objective of the whole discussion was to tackle the matter of communication with board members.

"Now how about the connection to the board?" he finally threw in, since they had covered all of the points listed and this issue had not shown up.

Callie quickly volunteered. "Well, obviously, the rest of us need to stay away from the board members and they need to stay away from us." As the in-house attorney, no one was surprised by Callie's tendency to see things legalistically.

"That just doesn't make sense, though," objected Mort. "Surely we're not putting a gag order in place." Mort and Callie often sparred, but always respectfully.

David jumped in. "I think both of you are right to an extent. Technically, there is no formal connection between the management team members—other than myself as CEO—and the board members. But we aren't saying they can never talk. It's just that 'direction' ought to flow down from the board through the CEO and 'information' ought to flow up from the staff through the CEO." He added the point to the master list.

Mort scowled noticeably. Francis, the HR director, had an opposite reaction. "I don't see what's so hard about that. I hardly ever talk to those guys anyway, especially since the board changed."

Insights from the Secret Formula

- Management team shouldn't spend much time talking to customers unless there are big problems—special arrangements with key customers are an exception

- We see a pattern of people doing "end runs" around the person or role above or below—STOP THIS

- Don't allow problems to come up to management team unless the next level of managers has been unable to resolve them

- CEO to avoid giving direct orders to staff reporting to others on the management team

- CEO needs to be more consistent in communicating board decisions to whole management team, not just some individuals

- Only CEO is "formally" connected to the board, not others on management team—so pass info through the CEO, don't accept orders from board members

"Yeah, but I need to," Mort retorted. "Especially with Eckstein on the board. We talk about finances every day or two, it seems."

"How's that working for you?" David injected, borrowing Trevor's probe in Dr. Phil style.

Mort thought for a moment. All eyes were on him. Callie could not resist commenting. "Duh! At least once a week you whine to me about how much time Eckstein is taking. How can that be good?"

"Well, he's been asking some really important questions lately," Mort replied with an air of defensiveness.

David knew that Eckstein was contacting Mort frequently, but he had not wanted to jump to conclusions about his chief financial officer. Mort's reactions, though, were looking very suspicious.

"Mort, one thing is obvious to me—you're spending eighty hours or so here each week. That can't be good for your family." David was hoping to keep the discussion alive to ferret out some more information. Still, he wanted to keep it light. "I'm not saying we need to sing a campfire song for you just yet, but we want you to be careful."

After a moment of awkward silence, Jerry started to hum a vocal warm-up and snickers erupted all around.

"Point taken, folks," Mort acknowledged. "With that in mind, could we adjourn now and let me get on to the work that keeps me here late?"

Hopeful nods appeared around the table and David realized the meeting had run its course. Thanking them for their time and wishing them all a productive day, he excused them. The meeting had not been everything he had aimed for, but he was optimistic that it was a strong start.

David spent almost an hour mapping out what he hoped to do at his next board meeting. This time, he was not going to allow Eckstein to hijack the agenda. And this time, he would lay his cards on the table. Better that he open the closet than be accused of hiding skeletons.

Simon slouched uncomfortably as he listened to his father. He was expecting another loud lecture, but this was going in a totally different direction.

"I make lots of mistakes, Simon. The mistakes I make with you and your mother are the most disappointing ones, because you guys are the most important people to me.

"One of my mistakes is letting my work prevent me from spending time with you when it would be best for you. Since work is not going away, I'll need your help figuring out when we can make things fit to best suit you within the demands of my schedule. What are some highlights coming up in your month that would be things I could put in my calendar?"

Hesitantly at first, Simon began sharing some upcoming priorities. He did not quickly flip to being a cooperative and communicative young teenager. However, the message was clear that his father was interested in making important changes.

David knew Simon would be watching closely for behaviors that either supported or negated the promised improvement. And David was determined to watch for opportunities to connect with Simon—to show his interest in his son, to reinforce his intended changes.

"Nancy, I know it's short notice, but I would love to take you out for a coffee and chat if you can manage it." It was nearly

9:30 at night and David knew that she rarely would head out at that time in the evening.

Call it women's intuition, but somehow Nancy was able to detect that David's invitation was heartfelt. Surprisingly for both of them, she pleasantly agreed. "I'm assuming we won't be too late. And that Simon will be okay."

With David's assurance, she grabbed a sweater and they headed into the garage. She chuckled as she slid into the smooth New England leather of the Z4's passenger seat. "This sure feels different than the minivan!" she exclaimed. It had never really occurred to David how rarely she had ridden in the Roadster. They definitely needed to get out more often.

For the first time in ages, the two of them had a great talk. To David it seemed they connected the way they had in their early dating days. He inquired about what was happening in her circles, specifically following up on some items that had been on her calendar recently. Then they talked about his conversation with Simon. Nancy was sincerely pleased with the time and care David was taking for family priorities.

Back home in decent time, as promised, they checked on Simon and readied themselves for bed. Resting nicely under comfortable covers, David was reviewing the positive strides from his day. Some greater openness with his management team. An encouraging connection with his son. Actual affirmation from his wife. Things were looking up.

But then he recalled the awkwardness of Mort's reactions about Eckstein. And that reminded him of his uncertainty about the agenda for the next board meeting. Worries gripped him again that night.

CHAPTER SEVEN

ONE STEP
FORWARD, TWO
STEPS BACK

.R. ightly or wrongly, the CommuniTrek board had a routine of meeting monthly for a few hours. David was beginning to wonder if this was the best approach. It seemed to him that he would just nicely get over one board meeting and it was time to start planning the next one. Surely there were more productive things to do!

Because he wanted this one to really work, he invested extra time planning what he would do and preparing materials to hand out. This time, he would provide so much information, Eckstein would not have a leg to stand on or a crack to squeeze through. April was conscripted to "pretty-up" the reports, copy them, and assemble attractive portfolios for each director.

David walked into his meeting, feeling certain that he had the upper hand.

◆◆

With the board meeting over, David returned to his office and collapsed in his chair with a weight of devastation. Throughout his career, he had generally had a feeling of confidence—even control—in meetings of his board. But now he felt like a juvenile. One of the new directors, Sarnacki, had inserted a question that was still ringing in David's mind: "Why are you telling us this?"

At first, it had seemed to David to be a stupid thing to ask—and maybe Sarnacki's relative silence at board meetings was because he was not as smart as people thought when they recommended he be added to the board. David had replied, with some condescension in his voice, that he always gave the board an update on key activities and developments.

Sarnacki's response had been as startling as a slap in the face, and in that instant David had despised him for it. "We know you're busy. But we only need to hear about results," Sarnacki had declared.

In retrospect, David admitted to himself that the tone of the statement had been neutral, even pleasant, though at the time it seemed to sting.

**Boards don't need to hear how busy the CEO is—
they need to hear about results.**

Sarnacki had commended the improved board packages that David had distributed. But he had gone on to explain that he would find even more value in a crisp, written report documenting progress toward the strategic targets and alerting directors to emerging issues. Gradually the rest of the board members had added their support, either verbally or with nods. Eckstein had asserted that he would be better able to contribute if he had a written report a few days ahead of the meeting so he could digest the information and mull it over. Muwanga had jumped in to say that he would need it a week in advance or it might not fit into his busy schedule. Again, there had been nods.

The discussion had continued in this vein, identifying several ways that the reporting to the board could be improved. David had not exactly liked what he was hearing—all he'd known for sure was that it would be taking more of his time. However, he could plainly see that the board was on a roll that no one could reverse.

He had scrawled some notes during their discussion and he was looking at them now. What was he to do with them? And how come he had retreated again from his intention to apologize to the board?

Rather than stewing in self-pity, he decided to call his coach.

"Thanks for making time to meet, Trevor. I've got a truckload to dump." David was still surprised that he was sharing his business problems with a pastor, but he could not deny that Trevor had been more help to him than anyone else he could imagine. He poured out his frustration about the meeting and his unmet objectives for it.

Trevor would have resisted the label "coach." Above all, he considered himself a friend. He listened intently. He shared generously. He encouraged boldly.

"Remember how we've talked about the board's job being to direct and protect?" Trevor asked.

David signaled the affirmative.

"And remember how aggravating you find it when Eckstein makes demands on your time or the time of your staff?"

Again, David nodded.

"The only way a board can responsibly do its job without meddling is by monitoring very well. So the reports that the board receives are absolutely essential to enable it to keep control without interfering. They ought to keep their noses in the business but their fingers out!"[1]

The only way a board can responsibly do its job
without meddling is by monitoring very well.

David liked the last statement but was still unsettled about the reporting burden. "Are you saying that the board has the right to demand any reports it wants?"

"Absolutely. But I know you're worried that this is going to put an undue weight on company time and resources."

"Right."

The best boards keep their noses in the
business and their fingers out!

Trevor leaned toward him. "David, you already think there is an undue weight. Eckstein is taxing your time. Maybe it's partly because he feels he hasn't got access to the information he needs to fulfill his responsibility."

"I don't know." David was resistant. "There's a malice to his meddling that seems to go way beyond fulfilling his responsibility."

"I've observed that people always do what they believe is the best thing to do in a given situation. Now, I admit, sometimes people are really confused about what would be best. However, they observe what has happened around them, assess the options, and act accordingly. Maybe Eckstein's doing the same things you would do if you were in his shoes."

David shuddered at the thought of imagining himself as Eckstein. "Can we just forget about Eckstein for now?" he implored.

"Sure. The point is, the board's not being unreasonable to ask for different kinds of reports. And it's totally understandable that the directors don't want to sit and listen to the CEO's commentary on the business for the whole meeting. Let's look at what they requested and plan how to improve things for next time."

"Why am *I* the one who has to make all the changes?" David used soft words for the self-pity he was feeling.

"Because as CEO, you report to the board. Because you're a leader and you want this to work. Besides, you're the one who feels most of the pain, friend. You have the most to gain and the most to lose."

Trevor's pointed response was a bit painful. And it was undeniably correct.

Resolutely, David pulled out his BlackBerry and, with
Trevor's help, made a list of steps he would take to reassure
the board members that they were receiving the information
they needed. He was hoping the steps would also enable him
to regain some of their confidence—as well as his own.

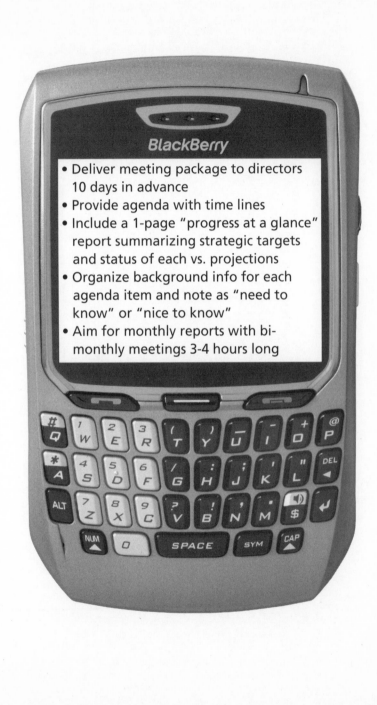

CHAPTER EIGHT

EXPECT MORE

avid entered his office, woke up his computer, and scanned his e-mail inbox. He double-clicked to read a message from Trevor:

David,
Every day had become a struggle for Archie. The smallest exertion left him short of breath. Headaches were common. It was a desperate day when he finally visited the doctor for a checkup. The prognosis was bad: Archie was suffering from high blood pressure and, considering all the other indicators, he might have only three months to live.

A month later, Archie was even more downcast. He had tried to make changes to his diet as demanded by the physician, but that wasn't going well. He had tried to exercise more, walking part way to work, occasionally taking the stairs rather than the elevator, but this only seemed to make him feel worse.

Overcome with a sense of futility, Archie decided to throw caution to the wind. Never in his life had he frivolously spent his money. Never had he really indulged himself. With two months to live, why not?! He decided to splurge and get a custom-made suit.

While being fitted, Archie heard the tailor reading out measurements to his assistant. With the tape around Archie's neck, the tailor called, "Eighteen and a half."

Archie reacted: "No. That can't be right. I always wear a seventeen and a half."

The tailor replied, "Oh, sir, you need an eighteen and a half—anything tighter will cause shortness of breath, headaches, high blood pressure, and even death."

David laughed out loud. Then he stuck his finger between his collar and his throat, wanting to reassure himself that there wasn't more to this teasing note than he first assumed. He breathed in relief, aware that Trevor was encouraging him to accept the change that would be required to move forward.

Although he was no closer to solving the mystery of who had been passing sensitive information to the board, David was gratified by some improvements he was seeing with the management team. His primary objective for the Secret Formula discussion had been to curtail inappropriate staff-board communication, but there were some other behavior changes that were pleasant surprises. Their meetings were much more open and productive. The others had become more willing to challenge his assumptions—in a good way, creating better decisions. They were supporting each other in the office. They were keeping the Secret Formula at the front of their thinking, insisting that they all operate along the straight lines of authority, accountability, and communication.

"I expect more from my board," David complained. He and Trevor had met for coffee and a talk, this time at David's home. David had quickly moved the conversation to his frustrations with his board.

"I understand that," Trevor replied. "But David, it's not just about what *you* expect. What do the shareholders expect? That's who the board really works for. And what do the board members expect? They have to be jointly committed to a role and a design for governing the organization."

David winced.

Trevor continued, "You react as if it will be impossible for the board to make good choices about this. Granted, you may have some of the wrong people on your board at the moment, but it's not as bad as you fear. The media have projected a paranoid notion that corporate directors are essentially lazy, selfish fools. That's rarely the case. Indeed, behaviors that give that appearance are more likely rooted in poor governance design than in the abilities of the directors."

"Wow, Trevor, you have such strong opinions on this. I have to admit that I've shaken my head more than a few times about coming to a pastor for advice about my business. Now I'm shaking my head again. What makes you so interested and opinionated about corporate governance?"

Trevor leaned back with a pensive look on his face. "I don't exactly know, David. I think it's just that I've always lived there."

"What are you talking about? You work in a church!" David realized how incredulous he sounded and immediately felt uncomfortable.

"Don't be so quick to castigate the church. The best churches have great boards, you know. Besides, I haven't spent my entire life as a pastor. My father was a CEO. I grew up wanting to emulate him; trying to impress him, even. I worked as a junior executive, turning heads and climbing the ladder."

David's eyebrows rose. "You are a man of many surprises. What happened to all of this?"

"Oh, that's a very long story." Trevor gazed into space momentarily. Making eye contact with David again, he continued. "The shortest possible version is that my father worked himself into an early grave, dying of a heart attack when I was twenty-eight. I recognized that I was on a path to do the same, and I made some major life shifts."

"You've gone through some hard times, Trevor," David responded, genuinely touched by what was obviously a much bigger story, with great heartache involved. "And now I'm even more baffled about your interest in the corporate world. It sounds like you wanted to run away from it."

"Losing my father was painful, and there are lots of things I wish I had done with him and said to him before he was gone. But redirecting my life was the best thing that could have happened. I believe it saved my life." Trevor spoke with calm conviction. "And I didn't run away from the business world; I ran away from patterns that were dangerous for me. I'm still very excited about business. I think I'd enjoy working in the business world. These days, I serve on the board of a national organization with a $20 million budget. And I'm on the Cedar Grove board. I keep my finger in those files—I just believe that my life purpose is best fulfilled as a pastor."

"You're on another board and you've never mentioned it?!" David smiled. "I'm shaking my head again. We started this talk with me bellyaching about my problems, and now I'm humbled with the reminder that in the whole scheme of things my problems are likely not that big. I kick myself again for not probing for more of your life story before now. It's deep . . . You're a wise man, Trevor."

"Well, don't get all mushy." Clearing his throat, Trevor spoke with a tone of authority. "You had raised some questions about your board and what you expect of it. It turns out that is another key to board effectiveness: the best boards are clear about what they *expect* regarding directors."

"You're changing the topic, but I'll let you get away with it," David observed graciously. "Let me see if I can pull this all together. You've said that the board's job is to *direct* and *protect* and they will be best able to do that if they *connect* and *expect*. Is that right?"

Chuckling, Trevor replied, "Just like a CEO—always zeroing in on the key points. You're right. And there's more to it— which we'll get to in a moment—but let's be sure we're clear about the 'expect' part."

"Okay. You tell me what I should know." David leaned back, gesturing with his fingers that he was ready for Trevor to pour it on him.

"What you should know by now is that I don't just tell you my thoughts—I expect you to think!" Trevor retorted good-naturedly.

David snickered. "Oops. I lapsed into 'feed me' mode. OK, here's what I think. I figure that if a board embraces its role as one 'to direct and protect,' then a lot of the confusion is eliminated. But there are probably some things that would be good to clarify regarding *how* they are to do that. For example, I expect board members to actually come to board meetings. Obviously, I have a couple of directors on my board who don't share my expectation."

Trevor nodded. "I agree that confusion is reduced by declaring the role, and I think the attendance expectation is a good example. What are some others?"

"Well, I admit that I have wanted the board members to pave the way for some new sales for the company, but I'm feeling guilty because that's not really directing or protecting."

Another nod from Trevor. "It's completely understandable that you would like any help you can get on growing the business. But you're right that this is not the true responsibility of the board—growing the business is *your* responsibility as CEO. However, that doesn't mean that you can never ask a board member to assist you in a key opportunity. The important thing in that situation would be for you and the director to realize that he's changing hats and becoming an agent of the staff. It's not a board responsibility. Recall the Secret Formula. He would be helping with the implementation of the strategy, not governing. As such, he would be under your operational leadership. This can be fine—occasionally—but some board members do not change hats well."

David nodded animatedly. "Since I discussed the Secret Formula with my management team, we've certainly been benefiting from keeping to those straight lines of authority, accountability, and communication. I've been careful to direct staff back to my managers so I don't interfere with their leadership. Boy, are they thankful. I wish I'd learned about that a long time ago."

Trevor was pleased. "That is encouraging, David. Any time we violate the Secret Formula, we compromise the organization's ability to perform.

"Okay, you gave me an example of what *not* to expect from board members. What is another idea for what *to* expect?"

It's the CEO's responsibility to implement, not the board's. If board members assist, they do it under the operational leadership of the CEO. Be aware that some board members find this difficult.

David pursed his lips and thought for a moment. "Well, there are lots, actually. A basic one is that board members come prepared for meetings. If I'm going to work to get all these reports done and sent out early, they better read them and be ready to discuss or decide. I think directors should put their thoughts on the table, not wait until the meeting is over and talk in the car on the way to the airport. I think they should let us know about any possible conflicts of interest. And they should protect confidential information—"

Trevor broke in, "You are on a roll, pal. These are all good. Some of them are actually legal obligations; others are just good practices. The fact is, when you put them all together you create a culture of the board. Every board has a culture. The problem is, most board cultures are developed by default, not by design."

"Wouldn't there be a list of all these good ideas somewhere?" David wondered aloud. "It seems like a waste to have to recreate it ourselves."

"Absolutely. I know of a few very helpful lists. But it almost never works to just accept a list. The best use of a list is to work with it as a discussion tool to expose the preferences and concerns of the board members. Passing a motion to accept someone else's list of ideas will not make it part of the culture."

> The problem is, most board cultures are
> developed by default, not by design.

"A lot of these things will just be common sense, though, won't they?" David pushed back.

"It's amazing how uncommon common sense is these days," Trevor countered. "Take your experience with a couple of board members who hardly ever show up at board meetings. Do you think that's because they are trying to disappoint everyone else or because they figure it doesn't really matter?"

"I guess I don't really know . . . I've never talked to them about it," David confessed.

"That just reinforces the point. Leaning on common sense leads us to make a bunch of assumptions rather than actually talking about expectations. Great boards are clear about what they expect!" Trevor said emphatically. "And great boards go even further. If board members don't do what they *expect*, the board takes action to *correct* them."

"Wow, these just roll off your tongue, Trevor. Direct, protect, connect, expect, and correct. This is really having an *effect* on me," David teased him.

Trevor laughed. "It's not rocket science. It just helps me remember what's important for boards."

"I agree—it's great, and I don't want to lose it—so give me a moment to add it to my notes."

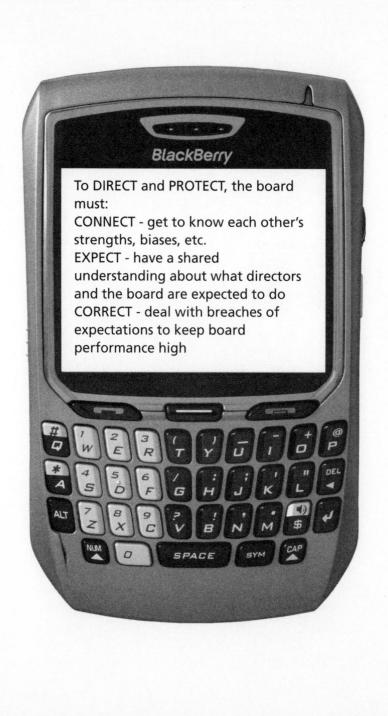

CHAPTER NINE

CATCHING
THE WIND

.A. lthough David felt a bit intimidated at the prospect of meeting with Chuck Sarnacki to discuss board matters, he had come to the conclusion that no one around the table had more influence on the board than this quiet, confident business veteran. Long retired from his post as CEO of a chain of retail stores in the West, Sarnacki remained highly active as a director of four other companies and a national non-profit. David had flown to Sarnacki's home base of Denver to make the meeting as convenient as possible for his board member.

"Chuck, thanks for meeting with me. I know you're a busy man."

"All you ever have to do is ask, David, and I'm at your service." The benevolent spirit that Sarnacki conveyed only made David more self-conscious for the ill will he had projected onto the director.

"Thanks. But I really need to begin by apologizing. I felt attacked at our last meeting, and I was reacting defensively. It probably showed."

Sarnacki smiled. "David, I decided long ago to try to never take offense. I meant no harm and I presumed you meant no harm. The fact that you are laying it before me just confirms that you're too big a man to wallow in self-pity."

David wanted to live up to the affirming words of this seasoned leader. "Actually, Chuck, I've been thinking a lot about the board—how I've been handling the connection I have with you and the other directors—and I'm not very proud of myself. Quite frankly, I tried to tell the board about this for the last two meetings and got derailed. Or maybe I just chickened out."

"Spit it out, son. There's not too much that can surprise me anymore."

Considering Sarnacki was easily twenty-five years his senior, David did not feel threatened by the "son" reference. In fact, somehow Sarnacki's nature led David to feel it was safe to be real. Perhaps he had become so accustomed to being real with Trevor that he needed to find out if it could happen with someone else, too.

"Do you think it's possible to manipulate people for the right reasons?" The question that came out had never been consciously formulated in his mind. Suddenly David felt very exposed.

"I think it's possible for someone to manipulate people to do what he thinks is best for them. And I think it's possible for someone to deceive himself about what is best for other people." Sarnacki sat calmly, his body language welcoming the exchange.

"Hmm. I don't know if that's good news or bad. Here's my story. I've come to realize that I tend to push my agenda with people—particularly including the board. I work with the management team to make plans for what we believe will be best for the company and I probably impose those plans on the board at times. I don't think I've ever forced something that is good for me and bad for the company, though." The pace of David's words had sped up considerably, betraying a defensiveness. "I just don't want this to create a problem with the board."

Sarnacki replied knowingly, "You play the 'ask for forgiveness' card rather than the 'get permission' card."

The fact that these words came so quickly to Sarnacki was unnerving for David. Yet having the core issue in the open was a relief, too. "I guess it was more obvious than I realized," he admitted.

"Do you think you're the first CEO to operate this way?" Sarnacki said with a gentle laugh. "Don't get me wrong. Just because it's a common tendency doesn't mean it's acceptable.

But don't beat yourself up too much. The question is, what are you going to do about it?"

"Well, I do have some ideas. In fact, that's what I came to talk about. I hadn't planned to bare my soul before you—though I'm glad I did.

"A friend has been helping me think more clearly about governance and I'm hoping you can help me even further."

Just because it's common for CEOs to ask for forgiveness rather than permission doesn't mean it's acceptable.

David laid out his understanding of the role of the board and the keys to making the board work. Sarnacki asked questions in a way that helped David confirm his own thoughts. As they developed a shared understanding, a plan for helping their board began to unfold.

"Gentlemen, thank you for making room in your schedule for this board retreat. As you've noticed from the agenda David sent out a couple of weeks ago, we have some different things planned for our time together."

At David's request, Sarnacki was opening the meeting. They had agreed that the topics that needed to be addressed would just unfold better if David was not the person to initiate them.

"Your premeeting package included an update on the company, and we'll get to that later. For our first item of business, we're going to benefit from the assistance of Trevor McAllister. His dad, Dirk, was one of the captains of industry while he was still alive. Trevor's going to help us step back and lay a foundation for how we function as a board . . ."

It had been David's idea to recruit Trevor as a third-party facilitator for part of the retreat. Sarnacki had voiced some reservations about using someone so close to David, so they had agreed that the three of them should have an exploratory meeting. He was soon satisfied that Trevor would not be a pawn of David.

During that first encounter, Sarnacki tested the "direct and protect" mandate—not because he did not believe in it, but because he wanted to be fully convinced himself. At one point, he proposed that perhaps the board's job is only to protect and to leave the direction-setting to the CEO and management who live in the context every day. As they talked this through, he acknowledged the potential problems with this. In fact, he ultimately declared that it was important to beware of becoming a "board of protectors." Emphasizing the "protect" role without fulfilling the "direct" mandate could lead to minimizing risks rather than maximizing opportunities while managing the risks.

Beware of the "board of protectors," because it will focus on minimizing risks rather than maximizing opportunities. Boards must direct *and* protect.

Many of the same concerns were aired during the retreat discussion, too. However, Trevor was able to play a facilitative role, drawing out the board members' thoughts—and drawing on Sarnacki when things were going sideways—rather than playing the "expert with the answers." This enabled the board members to reach their own conclusions rather than feeling imposed upon.

After a very productive morning and working lunch, the board played nine holes of golf. This was something that David had resisted at first, fearing that it smacked of the "good old boys" style of boards, which he was trying to avoid. However, both Trevor and Sarnacki had helped him see that there was a very deliberate purpose for the activity. The directors would be connecting—and doing so would allow natural follow-up conversations from the morning discussions.

They met for an early supper and reconvened for about an hour that evening to finalize their thinking about the role of the board and how they wanted to work together. Trevor agreed to write up the discussion notes so the board could later review them and formulate specific policy.

"I'm amazed how well it went," David exclaimed. He had picked Trevor up in the Z4 and they were on their way to a Cedar Grove board meeting. "The day you spent with us was incredible. And it continued. That night, all the directors hung around and chatted. There were some amazing stories of what some of the guys have experienced. And then the next day we had a great review of business progress. In fact, one of the highlights was an agreement to move to bimonthly meetings with interim reports, just as you and I had hoped for!"

Trevor grinned. "That's great. But you were still missing those two directors. Did you talk about that?"

"Yep. After we agreed the first day that 100-percent meeting attendance is expected, the board emphasized that these absences need to be addressed. Someone suggested we just ditch them, but Muwanga pointed out that they deserve an opportunity to be 'corrected' first. As board chair—and not as CEO, they reminded me—I will be talking to both of them in the next couple of weeks. Chuck has agreed to help me with that." David's rapport with Sarnacki had evolved so remarkably he was comfortable using his first name. In fact, it seemed unnatural to even think of calling him anything other than Chuck.

"Wait until you hear this, though," David continued. "After the business review, we talked about how the board could best work with the CEO. We added to your list!" David was sure Trevor would like their ideas. He pulled out his Black-Berry to show him the list as he spoke.

"The first key is that the board has to *select* an appropriate CEO. Obviously, many boards inherit a CEO, but it's still their responsibility to decide if that person is the right one to lead the operations going forward. And, on an ongoing basis, the board needs to monitor how things are progressing. For this, we used the word *inspect*, although it sounds a little too invasive. You know what I mean, though, don't you?"

"What a great addition!" Trevor tapped the dashboard. "I know exactly what you mean. The purpose of these word prompts is not so much to be precisely accurate by definition as it is to be easily memorable so we keep the keys in our minds. I'm impressed!"

"I've got even more news," David kept pushing, eager to relay everything before they reached their destination. "I feel like I've really turned the corner with Simon." He was grinning widely.

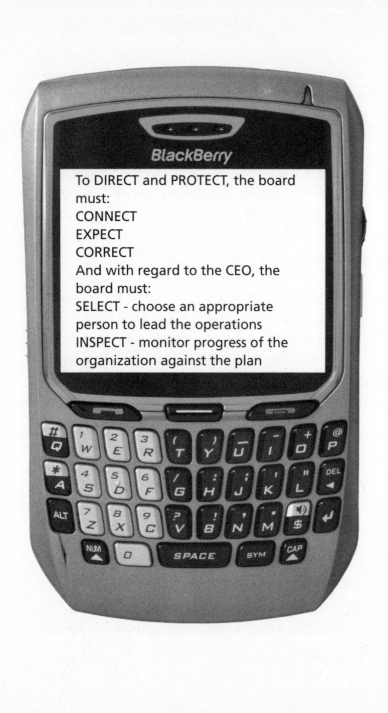

To DIRECT and PROTECT, the board must:

CONNECT

EXPECT

CORRECT

And with regard to the CEO, the board must:

SELECT - choose an appropriate person to lead the operations

INSPECT - monitor progress of the organization against the plan

"Tell me more," Trevor prompted him.

"Well, I've been using the keys for board relations in my relating with him. I've been deliberate to 'connect,' I've been careful to share what I 'expect,' and I've taken time to 'correct' when necessary. I'm still a bit clumsy at it, but it's working!"

"Wow, David, you really have the wind in your sails," Trevor said as David steered into a parking spot. "Let's hope this favorable breeze takes us through a productive meeting tonight."

CHAPTER TEN

UNCOVERING

THE GEM

.A. s David rushed back to his office from a meeting across town, he was reminded how fortunate he was to have a talented and committed
assistant. Having gone overtime at his engagement, he was
relieved to read an e-mail on his BlackBerry from April:

> Chuck & Trevor are in the meeting room. I've alerted them
> that you're tied up but will come ASAP. I'll keep them com-
> fortable—buzz me when you're nearby and I'll have Sandy
> meet you out front to park your car so you can run up.

As a follow-up to the board retreat, the three of them had
agreed to meet as soon as Trevor and David had each drafted
the reports they had been assigned.

"I'm so sorry to keep you waiting, guys," David apologized
as he entered the room and shook their hands in warm greeting. It was obvious that Chuck and Trevor were unconcerned
about the delay—they had probably found lots to talk about
for the fifteen minutes they had waited. Still, David had to
work at getting over being late for any appointment. Pushing
himself to dismiss his internal self-condemnation, he contin-

ued, "I'm really eager to see you both today, and I'm hoping you can indulge me before we get on with our official meeting purpose."

As Chuck and Trevor took their seats, they assured David that they were open to talking about whatever he had on his mind.

"Trevor, you've been telling me about these different facets of effective governance. It struck me that they all go together to make a Governance Excellence Model." David's enthusiasm was undaunted by Trevor's expressionless response. "In this Governance Excellence Model—or G.E.M.—each aspect represents a facet of a cut stone like a diamond—a gem. Look." David moved quickly to the whiteboard and began to sketch.

"A cut diamond has two sections—the top, or crown, and the bottom, which is called the pavilion. Each point has cut faces—facets. For our Governance Excellence Model, we'll show only six facets, though real diamonds have many more. On the top are Organizational Results, Owner Expectations, and Prominent Leadership. These are on top because they're the facets that everyone sees. Below are the facets that really provide the base or foundation for the upper ones: Organizational Performance, Board Relations, and Board-Management Interaction."

With interest and curiosity, Trevor and Chuck got up to join David at the whiteboard.

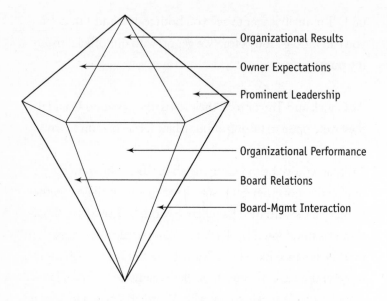

Organizational Results

Owner Expectations

Prominent Leadership

Organizational Performance

Board Relations

Board-Mgmt Interaction

"As you have both helped me understand, these facets are critical to any organization's success. And the board has a part to play in each." David began to list key points as he spoke.

"The glaring facet to the outside world is that of Organizational Results. Most board members are the way I was—so conscious that this part is most visible that they are tempted to try to shine up that surface themselves. But I'm learning that an organization is like a diamond—the most obvious facet will shine the brightest when all the other facets are properly in place, refracting light to it. If we've done our work in the other areas, we'll be happy with the appearance of this facet. The board's real responsibility in this area is to be familiar with the organization's results and understand the reason behind any significant deviations from the projections. Rather than reacting, directors simply *reflect* on these results, considering how they may impact the future plans and performance of the organization. Trevor, you'll recognize that I'm building on the pattern you have already shared."

Trevor smiled as he learned of another addition to the keys they had been discussing.

Organizational Results are a product of all the efforts of everyone in the organization. The board's responsibility is simply to *reflect* on these results.

"Oh yeah, everything rhymes with *direct* and *protect*," recalled Chuck. "I think *reflect* is an important key. If anything, there seems to be a tendency for boards to look at the numbers and act from them. It's kind of like they're driving a car with both hands on the rearview mirror rather than holding onto the steering wheel where the real direction is determined."

"What a great analogy, Chuck!" David laughed. "The connection to the rearview mirror is priceless. Boards are to *reflect* on what's in the mirror—the past—but they're to lead by what they see out the front window—the present and future.

"This is exactly why I want us to talk—I'm hoping you guys can help me flesh out the thinking on the G.E.M." David's enthusiasm drew knowing smiles from both of his friends.

"Another facet on the crown of this gem is Owner Expectations," he continued. "This is more significant than many board members acknowledge. For CommuniTrek, it involves the shareholders. But owners can mean members of an association."

Nodding, Trevor added, "Or, as with Cedar Grove, it could be the members of a community. In these cases, it's a matter of *purpose-centered ownership* rather than financial ownership. The group of people fully aligned with the whole purpose of the organization—or on whose behalf the organization was created—represents the most important ownership base."

Recognizing an organization's purpose-centered ownership clarifies how people would have an ownership stake in a non-profit.

"Hey, I like that concept of *purpose-centered ownership*, Trevor," commented Chuck. "It helps clarify how people would have an ownership stake in a non-profit."

He went on, "David, this area of Owner Expectations is a hot button for me. I think there's a lot for boards to be doing in this regard."

David grinned. "I thought you'd have some ideas on this. Tell us what you're thinking."

Chuck, who normally spoke with such calm confidence, now began to animate his points with gestures unlike any David had seen from him before. "Well, as board members, I think we're responsible to listen to the owners and truly understand their various perspectives. In fact, we ought to invite them to share their perspectives with us. We also have an obligation to report major decisions and results to the owners. And to help them understand what we've done, why we did it, and why our organization's results are what they are. The fact is, owners all have some expectations about how the organization will work and the results it will achieve. If the board isn't deliberately keeping its 'finger on the pulse' of owner expectations, distance may come between them. Then owners start to bail out."

Trevor probed further. "So, what do you think would be a word to communicate all those aspects of the board's responsibility?"

Chuck did not need a moment to think. Instantly, he declared, "The key word for boards regarding owners is *respect*."

Both David and Trevor nodded approvingly. "Hot button is right, friend," Trevor remarked. "You've definitely got some high-octane energy on this topic."

The key word for boards regarding owners and their expectations is *respect*.

Chuck poured out more of his passion. "The sad reality is that boards from every type of organization are suffering from an epidemic of self-importance. It's as if directors take their seat on a board and immediately assume they know what the owners want and believe. Amazingly, many directors don't even own shares of the company they govern. Board members seem to be willing to think *for* the owners, but—more important—they're supposed to think *of* the owners."

Trevor added to Chuck's theme with a provocative question: "Wouldn't it be shocking for a shareholder to get a note or a call from a board member, inviting input?"

David responded to both of them, saying, "Obviously, it's neither possible nor desirable to talk with every owner, but it's ridiculous to use that as an excuse not to connect with *any* owner. Besides, there are lots of ways to use technology to improve board-owner communication and understanding.

"I love what you're coming up with." Now David turned back to the G.E.M. figure on the whiteboard. "Let's keep this rolling. Just as boards ought to be conscious of owners' expectations, they're also wise to understand that who they put in Prominent Leadership positions has an impact on the organization. This is the remaining facet that's most open to the outside world.

"Chuck, on the second day of the board retreat, we came up with the key word *select* in regard to the CEO. But it occurs to me that the concept is just as critical for most board members and company officers. Certainly the chief financial officer's reputation can affect the world's view of a company."

"I concur," Trevor responded. "And if the chairman is someone other than the CEO, that person's reputation and behavior will be scrutinized by the world around them. And it's just as valid at non-profits. The chairman and the treasurer affect the image of the organization." He seemed to be relishing the elaboration of the keys to board excellence.

"This is all good, David, but sometimes the choice has been made and things aren't going so well." Chuck's tone was emphatic—apparently he was speaking from experience.

"The board shouldn't just wait until things get bad enough that it has to select someone different."

"Hey, I know," Trevor jumped in. "The board also needs to *redirect* their prominent leaders now and then."

"Even more," Chuck proceeded, "the board may have to *eject* a prominent leader at times."

Trevor chuckled at Chuck's quickness. They turned to see a very sober look on David's face. Everything went silent.

A twitch in the corner of David's mouth betrayed his ploy and all three of them joined in a boisterous guffaw.

"Chuck, I'm counting on your redirecting me so that ejecting me doesn't become a necessity." He began writing these new ideas on the growing list of points about the G.E.M.

Although David was laughing as he made his comment, Chuck responded with instant clarity. "Friend, you can count on me to help you succeed in your role . . . as long as you understand that it can never be at the cost of the entire ownership."

The board's role with its Prominent Leadership is to
select, redirect, and—if necessary—*eject.*

"That's all I would ever ask for, Chuck." David recalled the time when Trevor said he was always going to be his supporter—even if it meant disagreeing with him. David realized that, oddly, he felt safer because he knew he had people around him who cared enough about him to challenge him.

"Let's look to the lower facets of the G.E.M. Organizational Performance is the heart of the board's responsibility. Succinctly, we have come to see that the board's job is to *direct* and *protect*." Again he was writing points on the whiteboard as he spoke. "This involves defining and refining the vision, mission, and values of the organization. It includes determining the key result areas that will advance the organization toward fulfilling the vision and mission. It demands that board members grasp the breadth of the context in which the organization exists—their industry, their market, their community."

"Excellent summary of the *direct* side of this facet, David," said Trevor.

"I agree," said Chuck. "The problem is that in most companies, the CEO is seen as the person who undertakes all of this. And most CEOs are so highly motivated to lead their business that they take leadership in the direction-setting area. But this is best done *with* the board, not *for* the board."

"Amen, Chuck," Trevor responded. "In my opinion, the CEO is a functional member of the board. Certainly in businesses, this is the general case. But it ought to be true even in non-profits. Whether he or she is actually recognized as a member with a vote is not the issue. The CEO must be more than a hireling of the directors. The CEO will be fully effective only when he or she has a passion for the organization's vision and commitment to its plans. At the same time, though, I believe it's essential that the CEO and the board be clear that the board—as a whole—is the 'supervisor' of the CEO."

"I'm on board with all of your comments, Trevor," Chuck replied. "The Secret Formula you showed us makes this clear."

He turned to David. "On this point, there are some things about how the CommuniTrek board operates—and our structure—that we will need to talk about eventually. Without any criticism to you, it will be worth discussing your role as chairman. For our own effectiveness—and for compliance with recent legislation and pressures—we may benefit from separating the roles of chairman and CEO."

David was listening carefully. "I know you're not trying to mount a coup, Chuck, so I grant you that it's something worth discussing. It does press some buttons inside me, though, so I don't want any rash actions on this."

Chuck signaled his support.

Trevor picked up the conversation to bring it back on topic. "The other part of this Organizational Performance facet is *protecting*. Boards must develop a system and practices for monitoring the organization's progress so that corrective measures can be applied if they get off course. They're trustees on behalf of the owners to ensure that the organization's purpose—which is the motivation for the owners to have a stake in the enterprise—advances as much as possible. The most pivotal person in making progress happen is the CEO."

"That brings us to the next facet," said David. "Board-Management Interaction includes a host of responsibilities. The person the board selected as the senior staff person—whether that title is CEO, executive director, general manager, or whatever—gets delegated the responsibility of leading the operations to achieve the organization's aims. That expectation, and any other ones that the board has, must be made perfectly clear to the CEO. Which leads me to believe that the key word *expect* is essential in this facet, just as we've used it elsewhere."

Trevor spoke up again. "I won't argue with that. But I will point out that having worked with a number of non-profits, this is where there's often some resistance. There's a common concern that this puts too much weight on the executive director. Or, more often, the real concern is that it may put too much control in the hands of the executive director."

Chuck was the one to respond to this. "There are always risks in delegation. But delegation is the road to multiplied results. When we work together as a team, with every person playing their part, we share more victories. Think of a baseball pitcher. Like it or not, a lot of weight rests on that role. The wisest thing a team can do is select someone with great talent and delegate the responsibility to him. No sense having the second baseman running in to pitch every now and then. Likewise, there's no sense in a board trying to be the CEO. However, a CEO will have limited success if she doesn't have the support of the board team around her, just as a pitcher will do poorly if the other eight players on the field are not pulling their load."

> There are always risks in delegation. But delegation is the road to multiplied results.

"Okay, I can see your logic to overcome the 'too much weight' concern, but what do you say to the 'too much control' concern?" Trevor had his own answer but was keen to learn from the other two.

"Well, I can comment on that," said David. "The more I understand the board's role of directing and protecting, the more I see that most CEOs will have *less* control than they would otherwise. And I'm growing comfortable with that, because what it really means is that the CEO has less control over the

big-picture direction-setting. That will be safer for the organization—to be overseen by a board. Meanwhile, the CEO
maintains great liberty to make the calls on operational issues."

Trevor nodded. "Good. And I would add that for lots of
non-profits, they have the control lever reversed. The board
is very involved with operational details but tends to be
uninspired to tackle the big-picture issues."

"I say that the control question is a bit of a red herring anyway," Chuck contributed. "If the board is doing its job, its
concern will be progress, not control. It will have systems to
monitor results and compliance rather than relying on board
members sticking their fingers into the details."

Trevor and David looked at each other and chimed in uni-
son, "Noses in, fingers out!" They both laughed.

Monitoring the results the CEO has achieved compared
to the plans and policies set by the board is how the
board fulfills the responsibility to *inspect*.

Chuck looked at them quizzically, but gestured and sighed,
"Carry on."

"Alright," continued David, still chuckling. "We've talked
before about a key word for this area: *inspect*. But we don't

mean spying or nitty-gritty, detailed analysis. Just a deliberate monitoring of the CEO's results compared to the plans and policies set by the board."

"Uh-huh," Trevor agreed. "But for board-management interaction to be ideal, we need to incorporate some kind of encouragement for the CEO and management team."

"Okay," said David. "I've added it to the list. Is there another key word to communicate that aspect?"

The three of them stood in silent thought.

Trevor offered tentatively, "Well, part of encouraging is 'building up.' A possible word for that would be *erect*."

Again, there was quiet thoughtfulness.

"It's a bit of a stretch, but I sure can't think of anything better," said Chuck. "Note it down, David, but maybe we don't need a word for every little piece of this."

"Fair enough," said David as he wrote. Then he turned back to them. "Last facet. For Board Relations to be effective, everyone had better know and agree with the reasons they are there—what they *expect* of each other, just like we just added to Board-Management Interaction."

"Right," said Chuck. "And we want the board members to invite feedback on how well they're meeting the expectations and offer helpful feedback to the other directors. If need be, they ought to *correct* each other to ensure the board is functioning optimally."

Trevor picked up the cue. "Above all, they *connect*—get to know each other so they can work together productively."

David built on that remark. "And they communicate in a way that respects each other while challenging themselves to think outside of the box. They're careful to clarify the mandate and authority of any committees they create . . ."

The discussion continued for a few more minutes until Chuck interjected with new energy. "These rhyming words . . . I've been trying to put my finger on what they really are. I think I've got it! I think they are the *disciplines* of governance excellence. They're the things that a board must do—must discipline itself to do—to achieve the excellence you are referring to with your Governance Excellence Model, David."

The three of them sat silently for a few moments, allowing the pronouncement to settle in. Recognizing how powerful the metaphor of the G.E.M. was becoming, David marveled at what had just transpired. In under forty-five minutes, they had discussed all the core concepts of good governance. David felt confident that he now had a solid grasp of the big picture of board excellence. He felt more ready than ever to serve boards superbly and support others to do the same.

The G.E.M. – Facets and Responsibilities

Organizational Results   **REFLECT**

- Understand and think about the results of the organization's operations and the reasons for deviations from projections

Owner Expectations   **RESPECT**

- Listen, to understand owners (the shareholders or members)

- Invite input from owners

- Help owners understand board actions and organizational results

Prominent Leadership   **SELECT**, REDIRECT, EJECT

- Choose people with the skills, values, and credibility to fulfill their key responsibilities

- Ensure the officers and directors project credibility to key audiences

- Remove people from these roles if they compromise the organization's effectiveness

Organizational Performance **DIRECT** and
PROTECT

- Define and refine the vision, mission, and values
- Determine key result areas
- Create and use a monitoring system

Board-Management Interaction **EXPECT,**
INSPECT,
ERECT

- Articulate board expectations of the organization and CEO
- Establish and maintain the communication process between board and CEO, including confirmation of CEO performance
- Foster an effective team dynamic between board and CEO

Board Relations **CONNECT**, EXPECT, CORRECT

- Agree upon, understand, and comply with the expectations of each other as board members
- Create and follow a communication process within the board
- Contribute to an effective team dynamic within the board

CHAPTER ELEVEN

BREAKTHROUGH

.D. avid strode into his office extra early on Thursday morning. There was a skip in his step that had been missing for some time. He had some special plans for the latter part of the day, so he wanted to tend to matters quickly.

He sat down at his computer and was particularly eager to open an e-mail message from Jason, a rising star in his graphics department. Pleased with what he found, he quickly typed up a message for Trevor and Chuck:

> Guys,
>
> Thanks again for making time a few days ago to help fine-tune the documents going to the board. They'll be out today.
>
> I'm sending this separate note, though, to especially thank you for brainstorming with me about the GEM. I'm attaching a couple of illustrations that were developed late last night.
>
> You'll notice that the GEM doesn't include *every* element we discussed. Jason wisely challenged me to try to distill the key

points to the most important ones—so the graphic would be less complex and more easily remembered. Have a look and let me know what you think. Thanks.

With the top down on the Z4, Nancy's hair was blowing tauntingly as David wound the Roadster along the mountain highway. Her smile shone as she squinted in the bright sunlight. "This is so beautiful!" she raved.

"I'll say!" said David, but he was referring to her beauty, not the scenery, fighting to keep his eyes on the road. Nancy seemed to radiate warmth these days. She had a new spark

The Secret Formula for
Organizational Effectiveness

NOTE: The Secret Formula for Organizational Effectiveness is a trademark of Strive! Inc.

The G.E.M.
Governance Excellence Model

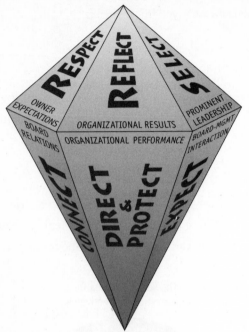

NOTE: The G.E.M. is a trademark of Strive! Inc.

and an unquenchable joy. In David's view, all of this made her more attractive than ever.

"We're almost there," he announced. They had booked a long weekend at a mountain resort and started out early that Thursday afternoon. They could have reached it faster by flying, but they both wanted to enjoy the scenery and the talking time by driving. Nancy's parents had happily offered to look after Simon for the duration.

This is going to be good, David thought. And then he corrected himself—it already was!

Tuesday morning, the off-site meeting with the management team had started according to plan. The six of them had spent the morning strategizing how to parlay a recent government contract in Africa into multiple contracts with larger corporations in the same region. For the last half hour or so, David had brought the team up to date on what had transpired at the board retreat.

"So, one of the things that I did was apologize to the board for my tendency to railroad our plans through to approval rather than giving the board an opportunity to question them and redirect us, if desired." David had talked about this enough now that he was not concerned about how people might react to his confession.

The management team was speechless for a moment. Erik, the chief technology officer, was first to respond. "No kidding? You just laid it out like that to them?"

"No kidding. The bitter reality, gang, was that they all knew it was happening anyway."

Callie, who was at most board meetings as corporate counsel, piped in, "I kind of suspected that was the case, David, but I was afraid you didn't want to talk about it. How did they take it?"

David winced within himself, but did not allow his reaction to show. *Good grief! She knew that the board already knew?* he thought. He was starting to wonder if he was the last person to know about everything around the place. He shrugged and responded. "Fine, really. They admitted that there had been times when they felt uncomfortable with the way things unfolded. The best part is that we talked about how we'll address issues in the future. Essentially, we agreed that new directions must be declared by the board before we commit any serious time or resources to them. How we tackle established objectives is our business as long as we keep the board informed and stay within previously defined parameters."

Jerry hopped on that. "Doesn't that mean that a lot of the plans we pushed past them probably could have been moved forward without even asking?"

"I would tend to think so," said David. "We haven't been clear about the difference between board and management responsibilities up to now. At times, we've taken plans to the board from our meetings and they were really the prerogative of the board, not management. At other times, we've asked the board for decisions on implementation issues. Now, we're all agreed that management should make those decisions."

The discussion continued and finally David broached the matter that was most awkward for him. "Remember back a couple of months ago when I took some heat at a board meeting and was accused of manipulating the audit committee?" he asked tentatively. Many of them nodded. "Well, something else happened at that meeting that has haunted me ever since. Ron Eckstein made some accusations and in the middle of them, he blurted out something he claimed I said. It was totally out of context, but it was a verbatim quote of something I had said at one of our management meetings a few days prior. I'm not on a witch hunt—I just want to understand what happened."

The next few minutes were definitely the most uncomfortable ones of the morning. Everyone sat pensively, not sure of where to look.

Callie finally broke the silence. "So what exactly is your question?"

"I guess I want to know who told him. Not because I want someone's skin—there will be no retribution. Besides, we hadn't even discussed the Secret Formula and straight line of communication up to that point. I just want to understand what I did wrong to motivate that action. 'Cause I want to make sure I don't do it again." He tried not to look directly at Mort, but he was dying to see how Mort was reacting.

The awkwardness persisted.

"That must've been me, David." All eyes turned in surprise and question. Jerry had uttered the admission.

No one was more shocked than David. Quietly, he said, "Okay. Can you help me understand why?"

"Because CommuniTrek is my dream, too, David. I've poured nine years of my life into this business and I was watching the new board members become uneasy with the way you were riding roughshod over them. I was afraid they might sink the ship because they didn't trust the captain."

Everyone sat in disbelief.

David spoke with careful determination. "Jerry, there is no excuse for how I acted with the board. I apologize to you, just as I have apologized to them." Various team members nodded to each other. "And I also want us all to have clarity about what we expect on this. No one talks to the board members about concerns they have with me unless they have made every effort to work it through with me first. Is that fair?"

Mort, Callie, Erik, and Francis simply stared. They could not disagree with what David had just said, but they were astounded at the directness. He had not shouted. He had not belittled. But he had not minced his words, either. They watched Jerry.

"You've got it, David. I'm the one apologizing. I joined this company because of the vision you have for the business. My dream is to see it flourish and I would rather see you at the helm than anyone else. I was acting in fear and I acted wrongly. I'm sorry."

"Then it's history. Lesson learned," David concluded easily. "You guys are the very people I want with me as we grow this business—and we are going to have a hoot! Now let's go to lunch."

Not fully grasping everything that had unfolded, they all rose and made their way to the hotel dining room. This would be a day to remember, of that they were certain.

As the server came to take their orders, David quietly got her attention and asked, "Ma'am, can you break this fifty? I'd like to give you a good tip today."

CHAPTER TWELVE

THE BIG DAY

◆ I ◆ t is strange how the most demanding times in our lives are often squeezed by obligations to unrelated activities. Tomorrow was the day David had long been anticipating and often dreading—the annual general meeting for CommuniTrek. Yet here he was tonight at another board meeting for Cedar Grove. In many ways, he did not want to be here. However, more than ever before, he was mindful of the responsibility he had accepted when he became a director. Plus, his appreciation of this little organization was ever increasing.

"Well, all of you received Cynthia's operating report last week, and the issues for us to discuss from it are noted on the agenda already," Amanda announced in her remarkably kind yet assertive style as chair. "However, there's one topic for us to discuss tonight that I believe deserves our greatest attention . . ."

David listened as she underscored the importance of the board evaluation process that they were about to initiate. He found it quite fascinating, and he was conscious of a flood of questions that were coming to his mind about the CommuniTrek board.

By the end of the evening, he was astounded at still another example of how his non-profit board experience was taking him into territory uncharted by his corporate board. The Cedar Grove board was innovative and ambitious and demanded high accountability. Corporate boards could hope for nothing more. Not only did his service with Cedar Grove help his community in tangible ways, but it was also sharpening his own skills and stretching him to be better at what he did every day. He was thankful that Trevor had encouraged him to persevere. And his thoughts drifted back to the CommuniTrek annual meeting.

As David paced around in the ready room beside the auditorium, his tension was high, but not overwhelming. In some ways he was more calm than he had been several months earlier. But then he reminded himself that by releasing so many of the details to others on his team, he was able to manage the pressure better. He could only imagine what last-minute problems must have come up with this important meeting's preparations. He savored the glorious realization that he was unaware of any of the problems—everything appeared perfect to him.

It was both gratifying and a bit unnerving for David to observe that almost 350 people had turned out for the first annual meeting. Apparently there was still enough interest in the company's future that an uncommon number of shareholders would take the time to attend. On the other hand, perhaps people's expectations of the stock's perform-ance had not been met and a horde had gathered to lynch him. He chuckled to himself as he remembered Winston Churchill's response when a friend asked if he was impressed that ten thousand people had come out to hear him speak: "Not really. A hundred thousand would come to see me hang." David shook off his doubts and reassured himself that his company had made important strides and he had some-thing that these people needed to hear.

"On behalf of the board of directors, I want to thank you for joining with us at this important gathering. Just over one year ago, CommuniTrek was launched on the public market. All of us made a commitment of hard-earned money with the optimistic expectation that we would be rewarded for our investment."

David had long ago learned that getting the first few sen-tences of a speech delivered with confidence was critical to its success. He had rehearsed those lines countless times, carefully perfecting the timing and the emphasis. He had said them so many times that the words would fall out of his mouth without his having to think. And then he said them some more, so that they started to have meaning again.

He now allowed himself to really see the people in the crowd, rather than moving his eyes over a faceless mass. They were watching him. They appeared to be listening, but they were still guarded. He would have to help them "open their gates" so they would really hear him.

"We're excited to report that our fourth quarter results have been strong and Year One projections for profit have been exceeded." He downplayed the fact that the projections had been exceeded by a very narrow margin. It had taken the better part of the year to clear up their board and management team confusion. Wonderfully, momentum was building, but David was conscious that shareholders had invested in CommuniTrek's *potential* last year—now they wanted results. Figures for Q4 and Year One were projected on the screen, generating polite applause. "Although we trust you're pleased with this announcement, we know that many of you are looking for even higher performance from CommuniTrek. Your board appreciates that. Every director has a significant investment in the business. We insist on that because we believe that board members must feel the impact of their decisions and their leadership as much as any other shareholder.

Board members must feel the impact of their decisions and their leadership as much as, or more than, any other shareholder.

153

"We have a vision for the future. When CommuniTrek went public, it extended an opportunity to the investment sector. It proposed the potential to develop communication technology that transcends political borders, linking people from any part of the world, regardless of their country's infrastructure. And CommuniTrek demonstrated its ability to make this dream a reality through the significant advances we made in our technology during the ten years prior to the initial public offering.

"Your investment," he said, and he began walking into the audience, calmly pointing with his open hand turned up, "and yours . . . and yours, is helping create the future we wish to live in. Your investment has enabled CommuniTrek to accelerate its R&D and production schedule. Enormous investments have been made in the future. And there will be enormous payoffs; payoffs in terms of enhanced personal communication around the globe and payoffs in terms of earnings for you.

"The future is bright! The board is assured that the management team has developed a business plan that will carry us to our destination . . ." Returning to the podium, David went on to give some highlights of the plan and to demonstrate how the company has already made significant advances toward fulfilling the plan. He could see from the body language and the growing intensity in the crowd that people were catching the message.

"Now," David raised his hands and paused. "I don't share these management details on behalf of management. I share them on behalf of the board." Again, he eased his way off the podium and into the audience. In quiet tones, he continued, "These details represent just a portion of the information the board members examine to ensure that all the shareholders' investment is being protected. And let me say again, every board member has a lot of his or her own money at stake, just like you. You see, the board is clear on its role. Its purpose is not to help the executive team figure out how to operate the company. The board's job is to direct and protect the organization as it fulfills our purpose in the best interests of the owners. We are here for you. The board's position is not management one step up, it's ownership one step down."[1]

David's energy and volume had built to a crescendo at this point, but he had not imagined what was about to happen. Applause erupted throughout the room and people were on their feet. He had received a standing ovation at his shareholders' meeting!

The board's position is not management one step up, it's ownership one step down.

"Isn't it exciting?" He lifted his voice and joined in the clapping. "As all of us play our part, we will realize our dreams.

Turn to a person beside you and declare, 'This applause is for you!'"

As the meeting continued, two new directors were confirmed by the shareholders. The truant ones had admitted their inability to meet the expectations, so the board had quickly done a thorough search for capable replacements. With another rousing round of applause bringing the meeting to a conclusion, David sensed a strange combination of both new energy and fatigue. He had prepared himself by expecting a favorable response at this meeting, but it had gone better than he had dreamed possible. Considering the changes he had made as a leader and with his board, he was anticipating a great year ahead. They had made huge strides on the path to governance excellence.

For the first time in a long time, David believed his nightmares were a thing of the past. Tonight he would sleep soundly. Tomorrow would be a tremendous day.

MAKING
APPLICATION

·H· ow did things fare for David and Communi-Trek in the end? I am partial to happy endings myself. I figure there are enough disappointments around me. Why would I want to read a book that ends with a downer?!

I have already envisioned a happy ending to your story, too. The fact that you read this book is a wonderful indicator that you are not satisfied with the status quo of governance in your circles. Good. Neither am I. And together, we can create a path to a meaningful, enriching future for the organizations we serve. In the following pages, I summarize the key elements of the Governance Excellence Model—the G.E.M.—and review the Secret Formula. In addition, I present some elaboration on each of the seven disciplines. As explained in the Introduction, we see discipline as something we *do*.

Therefore, I have included action steps and principles to serve as aids for you to improve your doing in each of the disciplines. I have focused these aids to address what tends to be particularly lacking among boards regarding each of the disciplines. I have tried to use examples that have application to any type of organization, be it for-profit, non-profit, or charitable. I often refer to the CEO, but the concepts are relevant, whatever title you use. Naturally, you will have to make some adjustments for your own context. Throughout, I share links for you to take advantage of more resources we offer online.

The Story Continues

Want to know more about what happens to David and Trevor? Follow-up chapters will be online in the months ahead. Simply sign up at www.imperfectboard.com/followup. You'll be automatically notified when one is available.

I trust that your energy and commitment, along with the information shared in this book, will enable you to activate and hone the Seven Disciplines of Governance Excellence. Best wishes as you take steps toward being a healthy board!

Board Boosters by BlackBerry

Visit www.imperfectboard.com/boosters to download all of the summary notes that David made on his BlackBerry. You'll have constant reminders of the key concepts for governance excellence. And you can add or edit as best suits your needs.

The Governance Excellence Model

Governing well is no easy task. It takes knowledge, skill, and experience. It takes courage and character. And it takes teamwork, in the sense of everyone bringing their unique talents and backgrounds to work together for the best interests of the people the board serves. The track record of board disasters over the past several years underscores how demanding board work can be. But even with all the challenges, it need not be complicated.

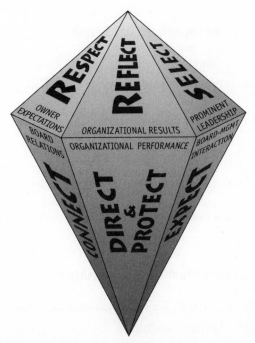

NOTE: The G.E.M. is a trademark of Strive! Inc.

The Governance Excellence Model illustrates the keys for
boards to do their part in making their organizations successful. Shown as a diamond—a G.E.M.—it has six facets or
areas of responsibility. There are disciplines associated with
each area of responsibility and these disciplines capture the
essence of the board's work. In the following section, I list
the disciplines and their associated areas of responsibility.
Some elaboration is provided for each area of responsibility.

Remembering the seven disciplines will best help board
members keep their governance priorities top of mind.

REFLECT . . . on Organizational Results

♦ Understand and think about the results of the organization's
operations and the reasons for deviations from projections

RESPECT . . . Owner Expectations

♦ Listen, to understand owners (the shareholders or members)

♦ Invite input from owners

♦ Help owners understand board actions and organizational
results

SELECT . . . your Prominent Leadership

♦ Choose people with the skills, values, and credibility to
fulfill their key responsibilities

- ◆ Ensure the officers and directors project credibility to key audiences

- ◆ Remove people from these roles if they compromise the organization's effectiveness

DIRECT and PROTECT . . . Organizational Performance

- ◆ Define and refine the vision, mission, and values

- ◆ Determine key result areas

- ◆ Create and use a monitoring system

EXPECT . . . great Board-Management Interaction

- ◆ Articulate board expectations of the organization and CEO

- ◆ Establish and maintain the communication process between board and CEO, including confirmation of CEO performance

- ◆ Foster an effective team dynamic between board and CEO

CONNECT . . . for healthy Board Relations

- ◆ Agree upon, understand, and comply with the expectations of each other as board members

- ◆ Create and follow a communication process within the board

- ◆ Contribute to an effective team dynamic within the board

The Secret Formula for Organizational Effectiveness

In every effective organization there are five essential roles: the owners, the board, the CEO, the staff, and the customers. The context of the organization may dictate different labels for these roles, but for the organization to be effective, the roles must exist. For sustained success, it is crucial that the organization (1) is clear about these roles and who fills them and (2) understands how one role relates to another. Removing or inhibiting any of these roles will cause the organization to suffer.

The Secret Formula is a graphical tool to help leaders keep their organizations healthy by maintaining appropriate connections between each of the roles. The model also illustrates several key concepts:

- The board is selected from among the owners, so the interests and motives of directors are most closely aligned with those of the ownership

- The board is one—a unit—and relates to the owners and to the CEO as a whole

- Regardless of whether the CEO and chair roles are separated, the CEO role is distinctly different from and subordinate to the role of the board

162

- The CEO is accountable to and in communication with the board as a whole, not simply to the chair or a committee

- The CEO role is a pivotal one, representing a genuine vulnerability of the organization and potentially becoming a bottleneck if the relationships are not well managed

- Even though individuals may hold various roles (such as an owner also being a customer and a CEO also being a board member), it is critical to recognize what role a person is acting in and relate to them in that manner

Furthermore, after observing countless organizations for over a decade, we are confident that following the straight lines of communication, authority, and accountability is the secret to ongoing effectiveness; ignoring or violating these lines creates chaos.

The Secret Formula for Organizational
Effectiveness is a trademark of Strive! Inc.

The Seven Disciplines of Governance Excellence

To help you raise the bar on governance excellence, the following pages provide explanations and tools for each of the disciplines.

DIRECT . . . Organizational Performance

The most fundamental discipline of a board of directors is to *direct* the organization for high performance. Directing is a proactive discipline, focused on the future. But an alarming problem exists with many boards: they refuse to direct!

There are likely many reasons. It may be that the board is determined not to meddle inappropriately with management's work, but this betrays a poor understanding of the distinct and complementary roles of board and management. In non-profits, the reason is often lack of knowledge—volunteer board members commonly feel (and are) ill-prepared to speak to strategic matters compared with management personnel, who are immersed in the organization and sector every day. The same knowledge gap exists between boards and management of for-profits. But these boards are also affected by the old-style corporate board thinking, which is to let the CEO run things the way he wants because that is how you would like the board to act if you were the CEO. (The fact that many CEOs served on each other's boards to perpetuate this is a part of the cloud over governance that is only now dissipating.)

Another reason boards have not engaged in the strategic leadership aspect of their role is that, frankly, it is very difficult work. It is much easier to approve a report and politely discuss some developments. That allows all concerned to get done and have a nice supper.

So either because boards abdicate their role in strategy or management apprehends it, boards tend not to direct. This leaves them little meaningful work. In this case, boards are *ceremonial*, giving the appearance of governing but really just rubber-stamping management's decisions.[1] We can be thankful that this is less common today. Alternately, in the interest of doing something useful, boards get involved in some of the minutiae because these are tangible; we can shoot from the hip, give some anecdotes of our own experiences with something similar, and then assure the CEO that he or she can feel free to make the decision with the added input just offered.

Just as dangerous, though, is the tendency to turn up the flame on the other half of the board's basic role. They become a "board of protectors." Regrettably, much of the recent legislation is pushing toward this. Although it is ridiculous to suggest the board should not be diligent in its protection role, if it increases its attention on protection and fails to play its part in direction, much harm will be done.

A board of protectors is ultimately a tight-fisted, short-term-thinking, prove-it-to-me bunch that lacks leadership. For this group, risks are not to be managed, but avoided. Bright-minded visionaries will quickly disappear from boardrooms because they are just too overwhelmed by the rules and limits. The paperwork may be in excellent order. But the company's future is flat-lined.

The fact is, *directing is an essential discipline of governance excellence.* Here are some steps you can follow to move toward healthy, meaningful engagement of the board in strategic planning. These points assume that a functional strategic plan is already in place, likely thanks to efforts by management in the past. Otherwise, a much more detailed process would be necessary.

Strategy Takes Discipline
Visit www.imperfectboard.com/direct to download this outline and to learn about other aids to make the most of your board's involvement in strategic planning.

- Acknowledge that the responsibility of a board member cannot be adequately fulfilled without a significant time commitment. Boards that expect only fifty to seventy-five hours per year from directors are doomed to exacerbate the gap between board and management knowledge and surrender real authority over strategy to management.

- Clarify the distinction between strategy and operations. The board will be involved only in determining the organization's vision, mission, core values, and key result areas, and their indicators of success. How the organization implements and achieves those shared expectations is the prerogative of management (within boundaries, of course).

- Agree that board and management will work together to develop the best strategy they can conceive between them. They will all understand it; they will all own it. Past plans will be honored, not criticized, and refined for the future.

- Refresh your understanding of the existing strategic plan by reviewing it thoroughly and comparing projected results to actual.

- Meet for an annual off-site session (allowing about ten hours, with an overnight in the middle) to reexamine the strategic plan. Avoid the dog-and-pony-show approach with management presenting a PowerPoint demonstration and deluging the board with facts and figures. Engage the entire group, mixing board and management together, with activities such as these:

  ○ Pairs discuss how the vision engenders passion for them or what could be added that would engender passion

  ○ Groups of three list what they like and dislike about the mission statement

- Individuals record actual examples of how they have
  seen one or more of the core values lived out by people
  in the organization

Each of these activities is used to generate a whole-group
discussion on the aspects of the plan being considered.
It may lead to draft revisions for further processing. The
aim, though, is not to do the wordsmithing but to create a
shared understanding of these fundamental directives for
the organization. With that groundwork, attention can be
turned to exercises examining the current situation:

- Post flip chart pages around the room with titles of
  trends (Economic, Political, Demographic, Tastes/
  Preferences, and so on) that are relevant to your organization and have everyone cycle around the room, using
  large markers to add their observations to each list

- Post flip charts showing the points that management
  has identified as strengths, weaknesses, opportunities,
  and threats (completed in advance of the session and
  shared by e-mail with all directors) and invite board
  members to add to or question items, based on their
  presession review

- Brainstorm with the whole group the greatest challenges they believe the organization faces in delivering
  on its mission

○ Groups of three or four at a table list what appear to be the few areas where the organization could focus its resources to most strategically advance its mission

Again, these activities quickly involve everyone in the process and establish a broader base of information and perspective from which to make group decisions. With an understanding of the current situation, meaningful discussion can lead to a group decision about the key result areas for the organization. From there, the task is to determine what will be the indicators of success and how they might be observed and measured:

○ New table groups of three or four list suggestions for what would be the indicators of success for each key result area

• Ultimately, a draft outline of strategy emerges. Management is tasked with processing the proposed changes with more staff and presenting a wordsmithed version at an upcoming board meeting.

• Prior to this subsequent board meeting, management researches patterns and projections regarding the indicators of success and relays the findings to the directors, to support a group discussion at the meeting.

• Together with management, the board discusses the proposed changes to the plan outline, finalizing the vision, mission, values, and key result areas; measurable targets for each indicator of success are then determined, based on past trends and future expectations.

• The board formally approves the strategic plan.

Richard Leblanc and James Gillies, coauthors of the ground-breaking research reported in *Inside the Boardroom,* state that ". . . it is the formulation and implementation of effective strategies that leads to not only the unlocking of shareholder value but ultimately the success or failure of the firm."[2] And they are adamant about the board having an active role in strategy development.

Strategic leadership—*directing*—ought to be how the board most adds value to the organization.

PROTECT . . . Organizational Performance

The board is responsible to protect the interests of the owners. Boards are assembled to act as trustees on behalf of the owners they represent, be they stockholders or members or taxpayers in the community. Owners have expectations about what the organization will accomplish. It is the board's job to oversee the organization so its performance meets those expectations. In other words, directing well is a fundamental way for a board to protect the interests of the owners. The follow-up to that is to ensure that the organization is progressing as planned and complying with board policies and legal obligations.

A significant aspect of the protecting role involves monitoring. Boards arrange for information to flow to them in reports.[3] By far, the majority are *staff reports*, which come through the CEO. *Third-party reports* are prepared by a neutral party at the request of the board. Reports from the external auditor are a well-known example, but surveys by outside firms and studies by consultants are other examples of third-party reports that can help the board stay on top of the organization's progress and compliance. Indeed, prudence demands that to protect the interests of the owners, the board will not rely on staff reports alone.

The third type of report, another method that avoids blindly trusting management's reports, is the *board inspection report*. For this, some members of the board are appointed to look into some clearly defined aspect of operations and report back to the board. An example of a good use of board inspection is interviewing several staff members to assess how closely the organization is following the board-set values. Perhaps the chair and another delegate of the board would meet with a dozen staff members and ask specific questions to assess compliance.

Non-profits often use this method of reporting to reduce the expense of hiring an outside expert to do the investigation. It is important, though, to ensure that the process is done properly so boards may be better off hiring the expertise. Nevertheless, there are some simple monitoring tasks—like confirming that directors' and officers' liability insurance is in effect and up to specification—that are ideal opportunities to use a board inspection report.

An example of where too many boards have shown gross negligence in their protecting role is found in the general public outrage at the amount of money being paid to some senior executives. Obviously, overpaying any staff person is compromising the ability of the organization to perform up to owners' expectations.

In for-profit companies, there is generally a compensation committee to address all issues relating to the CEO's compensation. Non-profits may have a human resources committee for this purpose; many simply leave this task to the board as a whole.

Regardless of who does the legwork, there are steps that best prepare a board to make decisions on this topic. These steps are valid for any kind of board and organization, but the degree of rigor will vary:

- Tie as much of the compensation as possible to performance. Despite what Woody Allen said, merely showing up for work is not enough.[4] This demands that the board be clear about what the indicators of success are for the organization.

- Constitute a committee to do the research to help the board make good decisions related to compensation. Write its mandate so everyone is certain about the expectations. Choose members carefully, confirming they have the skills and time to do the job properly.

- Ensure that the committee is fully independent of management (no paid employees, former employees, family members, direct contractors, or the like).

- Find out how other people with similar responsibilities are being compensated. Survey comparable organizations to assemble and update data.

- Augment your data with information from broader studies by third-party groups.

- Consider engaging an experienced compensation consultant to ensure you have the most current information and are up to date on best practices. Underscore that this consultant must be hired by the compensation committee (within parameters set by the board) and not associated with management in any personal or material manner.

- While these committee meetings may occasionally involve the CEO to get information about the business and understand his or her motivations, the vast majority of this work will be done without management included in the committee discussions.

- Hold an *in camera* session at a board meeting for the committee to present the findings and two or three options for approaching compensation, along with pros and cons for each.[5] Best-case and worst-case scenarios should be analyzed and included in the report. Discuss thoroughly; if the options propose a major change to the compensation scheme, agree that no decision will be made until a future meeting.

Remember that a best practice is for committees to make no recommendations. This illustrates how the committee can truly support the board's work without bringing a recommendation. Every board member deserves to understand and weigh in on this highly important decision.

- If major changes are being considered, hold another *in camera* board session, informing each board member to arrive with the options ranked. Make a chart for everyone to see the rankings. Discuss further, particularly if there are notable differences in the rankings. Consider how owners and the public would react if they were to see the details of the plan in the press—because chances are they will!

- Make a decision as a board about which option to implement.

- Assign the committee the task to formalize the compensation plan and present it to management.

- Ongoing monitoring of actual payouts and liabilities (pension, stock options, and so on) is the committee's responsibility, reporting at least semiannually to the board.

- The committee, probably with the committee chair as spokesperson, is also responsible to explain the compensation plan when legitimate inquiries are made; say, at the annual general meeting.

- At least annually, it is best for the committee to assess and give feedback on each member's contributions, ensuring that the requisite competence and independence are maintained. It is also advisable to ask for feedback on the committee's performance from the rest of the board.

There are no guarantees that a compensation plan will not become a lightning rod of controversy. However, by following the outlined steps with diligence, you are more likely to devise a compensation plan that satisfies and retains management and can also be supported by the owners.

Protecting – Eyes Wide Open
Visit www.imperfectboard.com/protect to discover key issues that boards chronically leave unguarded and to learn about tools to help your board protect the owners' interests.

RESPECT . . . Owner Expectations

As explained already, the essence of a board's job is to direct and protect the organization in the interests of the owners. It follows that being clear about who your owners are and what they are expecting is paramount to governing well.

It is easy to identify the owners of for-profit companies— they are the shareholders. Non-profits often have a membership who are the owners. Identifying the owners of other non-profits and social agencies can be more difficult. It is often helpful to think in terms of *purpose-centered ownership* rather than *financial ownership*. The group of people fully aligned with the whole purpose of the organization or on whose behalf the organization was created represents the most important ownership base. This helps clarify how people would have an ownership stake in a non-profit.

Communication with the owners of the organization is a critical responsibility of every board. All too often, board members fall into the trap of presuming that their own perspectives and priorities are a sufficient proxy for those of the people whose interests they represent. And often the magnitude of the owner base simply causes directors to resign themselves to the impossibility of communicating with all of them. But there are many ways in which a board can reach out to owners, sending an important message to them and revealing essential insights.

This list of simple steps is just one example of what any board could do to discover and respect the owners' expectations:

- Discuss the importance of owner communication and the objectives of undertaking a structured outreach.

- Agree on a few key questions to ask.

- Identify two people for each director to call:

  - One influential owner (investor with significant shareholdings or longtime, prominent member)

  - One other owner, randomly selected

- Report one to three key insights learned from each call, ideally to a person who will collate all insights into a written report for board members to receive ahead of the next board meeting.

- Prepare by reviewing the reported insights, looking for trends, marking points that stand out, and noting any questions that come to mind.

- Discuss at a board meeting, expecting each director to comment on some aspect of the findings.

- Determine at least one conclusion, be it a new insight or an understanding, that emerges from your interaction with owners.

- Share with each other some of the owners' reactions to your calls and how that might affect the organization in the future.

Added Value

For sample questions, sample reports, and a suggested discussion guide to make the most of a structured outreach to enhance owner communication as outlined here, visit www.imperfectboard.com/respect.

REFLECT . . . on Organizational Results

It is common for boards to react—either favorably or disparagingly—when they learn of recent results of the organization. However, rather than react, the best response of the board is to take time to *reflect*. A tool to assist with this discipline is a list of suggested questions that can be considered by individual directors and later discussed by the board as a whole. This is not an exhaustive list, merely a collection to spur your own thinking.

- What are the leading indicators of success or early warning signals of problems for our business or organization? How are we doing in regard to them?

- Are we measuring what matters most for our strategic progress? Or are the reports only about what is easily or habitually measured?

- How do current results compare to the same period a year ago?

- How significantly do our results differ from our projections? Why are they different or what enabled us to forecast well?

- Are these results surprising, considering the information and progress we observed leading up to this? If yes, why?

- How do our results compare with those of other organizations in a similar industry, sector, or context?

- How satisfied are we with our results? . . . with our growth? . . . with our profit? . . . with our service to our community? . . . with our adherence to our values?

- How has cash flow impacted our growth plans?

- What reaction or response to these results have we seen from our staff? From our shareholders or members? From our creditors or funders? From our competitors or others in the sector? From the public?

- How have our risks changed since our original projections?

- What assumptions did we make that may deserve reconsideration?

- Are there cycles or trends that we assumed would correct themselves that we now see have not?

- Given the results to date, what appear to be the key challenges our organization faces and how would I prioritize them?

- Would it have been helpful to get some outside experts to give us input or perspective when making our earlier plans? If yes, why and who?

- Are we satisfied with management's efforts? Why or why not?

There is a constant interplay among the disciplines of governance excellence. The fruit of the board's reflection on these questions will impact the board members' thinking and add perspective to how they direct the organization going forward.

That's a Good Question
Download to your BlackBerry a list of questions like this, tuned more to your own organization's context, by visiting www.imperfectboard.com/reflect.

SELECT . . . your Prominent Leadership

The people you choose to be officers and directors are very important, because everyone associated with the organization is affected by the results these prominent leaders achieve and the impressions they project. Strong, confident, competent leaders enhance the organization and its potential for the future. People of questionable ability or character undermine future opportunities.

This discipline encompasses a range of board responsibilities. Obviously, it is critical for the board to select great leaders, and none is more prominent than the CEO. Whether the process for selection was robust or random, situations arise in which one of these people seems to be missing the mark. Then it may be necessary to redirect them, reminding them clearly of what you expect. And in a worst-case scenario, the board may have to remove or eject an officer or director from the organization.

Boards are notoriously poor at dealing with underperforming directors. Using this problem as an example to help you with this aspect of this discipline, here is a brief road map for you to use in taking responsibility in this area:

1. Ensure that your organization has a written list of expectations for board members. Without this common understanding, it is unreasonable to try to hold someone accountable.

2. Ensure that your board has decided under what circumstances, and through what process, board members can be removed from their positions. Then the person who is charged with holding peers accountable will be implementing an organizational policy, not imposing a personal preference.

3. Clarify who is the lead person responsible for holding the directors accountable on behalf of the board—common and appropriate options include the board chair or the chair of a governance or board development committee.

4. Encourage the lead person to express concern about the individual's behavior privately and quickly. Deal with the problem when it is small, before it gets out of hand. If the problem is verified as a serious breach of the code of ethics, it is important to take immediate action: proceed to step 7.

5. Determine what types of developmental support the organization will provide to help the director fulfill the expectations.

6. Explain the consequences of continuing to violate expectations.

7. Follow through on the consequences of not fulfilling board member expectations, carefully documenting the

steps that have been taken. (Believe it or not, there have been successful lawsuits for wrongful dismissal of a volunteer!)

8. Remove board members from office if they are not prepared or able to contribute appropriately to the team. If it becomes apparent that the officer will have to be removed, conduct an *in camera* board meeting to discuss and formalize the decision.

A group is only as strong as its weakest link. Disciplining out-of-line board members—and removing them, if necessary—is a must if the board is to lead the organization effectively.

Getting Everyone on the Same Page
To help ensure that everyone at the board table is aware of and committed to the expectations of all board members, visit www.imperfectboard.com/select to download our model leadership covenant.

EXPECT . . . great Board-Management Interaction

Great board-management interaction is vital for governance excellence and organizational success. It is helpful for us to remember that lots of organizations thrive with talented CEOs and dysfunctional boards, but no organization does well for long with an ineffective CEO. Supporting the CEO to success is an essential responsibility of the board. This begins by *expecting* the best from the CEO and articulating these expectations clearly. Fostering open communication between the board and management is critical. As well, it is imperative to develop and use systems to deliberately monitor the performance of the CEO compared to the plans and policies set by the board. And encouraging the CEO—with praise and tangible rewards—rounds out the aspects of this discipline.

Central to the *expecting* discipline is a written outline of the senior executive's job. Just what is this person supposed to do in your organization, anyway? At Strive!, we have lost count of the number of organizations in which there is no clear expression of the role of the CEO (or executive director or general manager or whatever the title). Worse, it is surprising how many organizations have no clear role description, yet have fired the person in the position! Performance management is one of the chronic weaknesses of boards of every type.

The Power of Policy
The best way to be sure that expectations of the CEO are clear and mutually understood is to develop written policies. These should not be terribly lengthy, but developing them can still take a lot of time if starting from scratch. Discover an inexpensive tool to catapult you forward on this task at www.imperfectboard.com/expect.

The "supervisor" of the CEO is the board as a whole, shown graphically in the Secret Formula (see Chapter Eleven). Regrettably, performance management is shrouded with negative connotations and bad experiences. As a consequence, most boards ignore this responsibility or abdicate it to the board chair, who may or may not do anything about it. Even if he or she does act, the most the board generally hears about it is that it happened.

Here are some thoughts and steps to help the board master performance management and improve the discipline related to board-management interaction:

- The key is to approach performance management with an intent to help the CEO be more successful. It is not initiated as a means of catching the person doing something wrong.

- Realize that your CEO is likely longing to hear what the board thinks of his or her performance. As author Ken Blanchard says, "Feedback is the breakfast of champions."

- Attempting to give performance feedback without a clear articulation of what performance is expected is indefensible. We define the CEO's job very simply: achieve the organization's goals within the board-set policies.[6] Put another way, the job is to fulfill the strategic plan without violating the values or boundaries the board has affirmed.

- Performance feedback is about performance. Not activity. Not intention. And evaluating the performance of a CEO is very different from reviewing some other employee's performance. The board is not assessing the specific tasks the CEO accomplished by him- or herself, but is really assessing the performance of the entire organization, because the CEO's job is to lead operations to achieve the desired strategic results.

- Performance is simply the progress of the organization toward the targets for each key result area (KRA) and compliance with the operational limits[7] (OLs) or boundaries agreed to by board and management.

- The board ought to have received regular reports (at least quarterly) that indicate actual results compared with projections for each strategic result area. This is the basis of your assessment. Techniques should be employed to ensure that the reports presented by management accurately reflect the progress.

- Have each board member, the CEO, and several others on the management team complete a survey assessing performance of the organization. An abbreviated chart to illustrate this may look like the example shown on the next page.

- All feedback is collated into a single report that goes *confidentially* to the board members (not the CEO).

CommuniTrek - David Slater, CEO - Performance Review	
Assessment Factor/Comments	*Rating*
KRA 1: Increase sales in each of the 5 markets.	
Comments	
KRA 5: Penetrate a new market.	
Comments	
OL 1: Prudent management of operations.	
Comments	
OL 9: Treatment of customers.	
Comments	
One accomplishment you would underscore:	
One suggestion you offer:	
Other comments you wish to make:	

- The board meets *in camera* to discuss the feedback, getting clarification as needed. Through discussion, the board distills the feedback into a single rating for each KRA and OL and only comments that are supported and understood by the board are retained. The objective is to develop a report that reflects the board's shared opinion of the CEO's performance. The board speaks with *one voice*.

- Two or three board members—including and led by the board chair—meet to convey the board feedback, discussing it in comparison with the CEO's perspective, emphasizing praise where it is due, underlining concerns, and agreeing on any professional development plans for the CEO.

- A summary report of that meeting goes to the board.

Performance Management in the Twenty-First Century
Take advantage of the power of technology to simplify the implementation and increase the impact of performance management in your organization. Use a system that

- Enables all respondents to enter their ratings and comments from the comfort and privacy of their own homes or offices, using an Internet link that is password-protected

- Ensures anonymity, to give each person more confidence to give feedback with candor and in detail

- Generates reports that collate and compare ratings, so you can see what feedback board members gave the CEO, what assessment the CEO gave her- or himself, and what feedback was given by the CEO's direct reports

Visit www.imperfectboard.com/expect to learn more.

CONNECT . . . for healthy Board Relations

The best boards work together as a team, capitalizing on the strengths that each director brings to the table and demanding full engagement by everyone. David Nadler described this well in his *Harvard Business Review* article: "The key to better corporate governance lies in the working relationships between boards and managers, in the social dynamics of board interaction, and in the competence, integrity and constructive involvement of individual directors."[8]

The *connecting* discipline demands that directors move well beyond the polite, occasional meetings that used to characterize board work. Board members function most effectively together when they understand what each can contribute and they challenge each other to bring their best. This requires mutual respect and trust. And this takes time. It also involves clarifying the expectations that board members have of each other and correcting each other when those expectations are breached.

To offer just one example of how a board can better connect, we can look to improving interaction within the board meeting.

I have long observed that from an energy perspective the typical board meeting is calm, ordered, and relatively flat. How disappointing! One would expect that people who agree to serve on the board of directors have an earnest interest in the enterprise and are eager to give their best energy and thinking in support of its success.

A simple way of waking ourselves from this veritable slumber is to employ some structure that transforms the interaction among directors in the boardroom. In Chapter Two, David and Trevor briefly discuss this happening in the Cedar Grove meeting under Amanda's leadership. Here are the steps you could follow to achieve the same results:

- To expose the perspectives that each board member brings to the meeting, select an agenda item that deserves full discussion; for example, a proposal for the organization to offer a new service.

- Ask all board members to stand, take a pen and paper, and find a partner from the other side of the table.

- Inform them that they have three minutes to remain standing in their pairs and list all the pros and cons that come to mind regarding the proposal.

- When time is up or when discussion wanes, invite them to sit beside their partner at the table.

- Gather and record the ideas, asking each pair to share only one pro in a short phrase, perhaps one to five words. (This assumes your board is an appropriately manageable size—say, no more than twelve members.) When each pair has contributed, ask if there are any other pros not yet shared and complete the master list. It is important to lead the time of sharing in a way that demonstrates you are interested in everyone's ideas.

- Repeat this process to make a master list of the cons. By this time, each board member will have verbalized his or her thoughts and be more ready than ever to engage in deeper discussion.

- Ask if anyone has questions or needs an explanation of any of the pros. Discuss them one at a time, as items are highlighted. Feel free to ask questions yourself, to generate discussion on any pros that seem to merit elaboration.

- Repeat for the cons.

- By this point, the board may be ready to make an informed decision on the proposal, having heard everyone's perspectives.

Double Your Money!

Raise the bar on this discipline with a new tool that gives you feedback on how your board is doing on all seven disciplines. The G.E.M. Assessment for Boards allows all of you to rate effectiveness on forty board behaviors and generates a detailed report with tips for improvement. Find out more at www.imperfectboard .com/connect and claim a discount worth more than twice the price of this book!

RECOMMENDED READING ON GOVERNANCE

◆S◆ helves are beginning to sag with all the emerging books about governance. Of the many available, some are better than others. I recommend the following books, and I have highlighted in boxes two that I think are outstanding.

Boards at Work: How Corporate Boards Create Competitive Advantage. Ram Charan. 1998. Jossey-Bass, San Francisco.

Boards That Deliver: Advancing Corporate Governance from Compliance to Competitive Advantage. Ram Charan. 2005. Jossey-Bass, San Francisco.

Boards That Make a Difference: A New Design for Leadership in Nonprofit and Public Organizations. John Carver. 1990, 2nd ed. 1997, 3rd ed. 2006. Jossey-Bass, San Francisco.

Called to Serve: Creating and Nurturing the Effective Volunteer Board. Max De Pree. 2001. Eerdmans, UK.

Corporate Boards: Strategies for Adding Value at the Top. Jay A. Conger, Edward E. Lawler III, and David L. Finegold. 2001. Jossey-Bass, San Francisco.

Corporate Boards That Create Value. John Carver and Caroline Oliver. 2002. Jossey-Bass, San Francisco.

Corporate Governance. 1995. Robert A. G. Monks and Nell Minow. Blackwell Publishers, Oxford, UK.

Excellence in the Boardroom: Best Practices in Corporate Directorship. William A. Dimma. 2002. Wiley Canada, Mississauga, ON.

Inside the Boardroom: How Boards Really Work and the Coming Revolution in Corporate Governance. Richard Leblanc and James Gillies. 2005. Wiley Canada, Mississauga, ON.

Reinventing Your Board. John Carver and Miriam Carver. 1997, revised edition 2006. Jossey-Bass, San Francisco.

Sarbanes-Oxley and the Board of Directors: Techniques and Best Practices for Corporate Governance. Scott Green. 2005. Wiley, Hoboken, NJ.

The Strategic Board: The Step-by-Step Guide to High-Impact Governance. Mark Light. 2001. Wiley, Hoboken, NJ.

Tougher Boards for Tougher Times: Corporate Governance in the Post-Enron Era. William A. Dimma. 2006. Wiley Canada, Mississauga, ON.

NOTES

Introduction

1. Ram Charan. *Boards That Deliver.* 2005. Jossey-Bass, San Francisco.

2. William A. Dimma. *Tougher Boards for Tougher Times.* 2006. Wiley Canada, Mississauga, ON.

3. Patrick Lencioni. *The Four Obsessions of an Extraordinary Executive.* 2000. Jossey-Bass, San Francisco. Pages xiv–xvi.

4. John Carver. *Boards That Make a Difference: A New Design for Leadership in Nonprofit and Public Organizations.* 1990. Jossey-Bass, San Francisco.

5. Adrian Cadbury. Foreword in John Carver and Caroline Oliver, *Corporate Boards That Create Value.* 2002. Jossey-Bass, San Francisco. Pages xiii–xiv.

Chapter One

1. Complaining that I don't understand someone who doesn't listen to me is ridiculous when I realize that my understanding requires me to listen to him, not the other way around. This insight comes from the wisdom of Dr. Stephen R. Covey on a tape set that was a precursor to his inspiring book, *The 7 Habits of Highly Effective People.*

Chapter Two

1. This vignette is inspired by a real-life story recounted by John Maxwell, an unknowing leadership mentor of mine for nearly two decades. He was visiting a restaurant for some quality time with his son Joel Porter—just a young boy at the time—and encountered an unpleasant waitress. John cannot resist lifting people higher, so he helped the waitress get an entirely new view on her day by changing her expectations with a paradigm shift.

Chapter Three

1. My colleagues and I were introduced to the concept of the board serving owners and staff serving customers during presentations by John Carver in the early 1990s. We developed our Secret Formula for Organizational Effectiveness as a visual tool to clarify the key roles and their relationships in any organization with a board. We have since discovered that John has employed a similar schematic since the 1980s.

2. John Carver has advocated the "one voice" principle as a tool to encourage dissent during discussion at board meetings and, simultaneously, not detract from the indisputably authoritative "voice" of the vote.

Chapter Four

1. A handwritten letter by President Lincoln, preserved in the Library of Congress, states that, "This letter will certify that Roswell McIntyre is to be readmitted into the New York Cavalry. When he serves out his required enlistment, he will be freed of any charges of desertion." He wrote it in response to an appeal by McIntyre's mother after she learned that her son had panicked and run away from a battle for which he was not trained to fight. He had been court-martialed and condemned to be shot for desertion. McIntyre's mother pleaded that he was

young and inexperienced and he needed a second chance. The generals, however, urged the president to enforce discipline. In their opinion, exceptions would undermine the discipline of an already demoralized army.

Lincoln thought and prayed. Then he wrote the famous statement, "I have observed that it never does a boy much good to shoot him."

Beside the letter on display in the Library of Congress is a note which reads, "This letter was taken from the body of Roswell McIntyre, who died at the battle of Little Five Forks, Virginia."

2. The comic-strip character Pogo, created by Walt Kelly, is famous for having said, "We have met the enemy and he is us." It appeared in an Earth Day 1971 cartoon strip and has spawned many similar sayings.

3. Michael LeBoeuf. *The Greatest Management Principle in the World*. 1985. Putnam, New York.

Chapter Five

1. This approach to committee work was introduced by John Carver to preserve the authority of the board to make governing decisions while still allowing helpful committee output.

Chapter Seven

1. Interview with author, July 8, 2004. Jim Estill is a CEO and has experience on several corporate boards.

Chapter Twelve

1. John Carver, at the International Symposium on Policy Governance in Toronto in 2000, shared this phrase. Fortunately, he

has included this important thought and elucidated so much
more in the 2002 book *Corporate Boards That Create Value*,
coauthored with Caroline Oliver.

Afterword

1. The wonderfully descriptive label *ceremonial* comes from Ram
   Charan, in *Boards That Deliver*.

2. Richard Leblanc and James Gillies. *Inside the Boardroom*. 2005.
   Wiley Canada, Mississauga, ON. Page 148.

3. John Carver conceptualized this reporting in three distinct
   pathways and used the terms *internal reports*, *external reports*,
   and *direct inspection reports*.

4. In their book *In Search of Excellence*, Tom Peters and Robert
   Waterman quoted Woody Allen as saying, "Eighty percent of
   success is showing up."

5. The term *in camera* refers to a meeting kept private or confined
   to those intimately concerned. In our context, this is generally a
   meeting of board members without any employees present. In
   some regions, people use the term *executive session* to mean the
   same thing.

6. Although our approach does not adhere in all ways to John
   Carver's Policy Governance® model, the idea of couching board
   expectations of the CEO in terms of accomplishing a job within
   boundaries of permissibility was first introduced by John.

7. Our use of operational limits or boundaries is roughly equiva-
   lent to what John Carver called 'executive limitations'—policies that describe the board-stated limits of acceptability within
   which the CEO must operate.

8. David A. Nadler. "Building Better Boards," *Harvard Business
   Review* 82:5. 2004. Page 102.

ACKNOWLEDGMENTS

This book is the fruit of many people's labor. I am blessed to be surrounded by talented, encouraging supporters. Wonderfully, the team at Strive! is second to none. My thanks go out to Cathie, Ralph, Mary Lynn, April, and Jennifer. And though Jenny has moved on to new chapters in her life, I appreciate the hope she spoke into this project when it was just beginning. You guys are the greatest!

I wonder if anyone writes a book during normal work hours. I certainly haven't! So it has been possible only with the support, sacrifice, and understanding of my family. Thank you Karen, my tireless cheerleader and life partner. Your dedication to our marriage and our children makes every day more joyful and more secure. And thanks to our children, Jason,

Sarah, Jonathan, Owen, and Peter. You add vibrant color to
my days and point to exciting possibilities for the future.

Several close friends and family members endured earlier
versions of this book, reading and reviewing and creatively
contributing to the final edition. Katie, your energetic input
has been pivotal. Andrew, your feedback is so appreciated.
Special thanks also to Pastor Steve Fleming, Erik Vander Ahe,
Larry Wood, Gary Schwammlein, Curt Hammond, Paul
Hubert, Wayne Johnson, Tom Schmidt, Don Moore, Ben
Kubassek, Will Tyler, Earl Pitts, Jamie Kubassek, Doug Vicic,
and John Pellowe.

One of the most unexpected experiences in this writing
project has been receiving such unreserved assistance from so
many clients, contacts, and other authors. Patrick Lencioni,
who has walked this trail before me, generously shared his
experiences and insights, but even more, became a great
friend. Thank you, Pat. And thank you to his entire team—
Amy, Jeff, Tracy, Karen, Michele, and Lynne—your openness and expertise have been remarkable.

I'm grateful for the help and encouragement from John
Beckett, Scott Green, Ken Blanchard, Nancy Jordan, Kevin
McCarthy, and Ram Charan. Jim Estill has given a stream of
valuable ideas and important contacts. Thank you, everyone.

Great thanks go to Sealy and Jeana at Yates & Yates. Thank you for believing in this book and agreeing to represent me as my agent. Your experience has been invaluable. Your mentoring has been a gift. Your patience has been a steadying force. And thank you to Susan Williams and the team at Jossey-Bass in San Francisco.

Most of all, I give thanks to God, who gives meaning and purpose to all my life. Everything I am and do is dedicated to you.

—*Jim Brown*

YOUR NEXT STEP TO A HEALTHY BOARD

Strive!
195 Janefield Avenue
Guelph, Ontario, Canada
N1G 2L5

Strive!
8888 Bank Road
Vermilion, Ohio, USA
44089

THE AUTHOR

JIM BROWN is a founding partner of Strive!, a leadership development firm that specializes in governance. With offices near Toronto and Cleveland, Jim and the team at Strive! provide coaching and consulting services to boards and leaders across North America and in various countries around the world, including Austria, Romania, Slovakia, Hungary, and Croatia.

Jim has coached key leaders from scores of prominent organizations, walking with them as they overcome the difficulties of structural reorganization, ambiguity in strategy, constitutional malaise, and a myriad of other challenges. His passion is to see board members and senior staff working together as a confident, competent team. And he always has fun doing it!

A popular speaker at conferences and annual general meetings, Jim brings experience with a practical understanding of boards and organizational leadership.

Jim has a master's degree in economics and personally serves on boards at the local and the national level. He lives outside of Toronto with his wife, Karen, and five active children.

To learn more about Jim, Strive!, and the products and services they offer, please visit www.strive.com or call them at 519-766-9033.

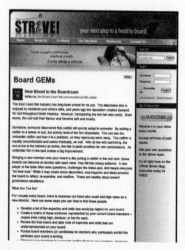

Board GEMs—*free* monthly e-bulletin

GEM Assessment for Boards